EUROPE IN TRANSITION

Series Editor: Steve Frampton

The Yorkshire Region

Bob Hordern

Hodder & Stoughton

A MEMBER OF THE HODDER HEADLINE GROUP

Dedication

Europe in Transition: The Yorkshire Region

I am pleased to have produced this, the third volume in the series, and am very grateful for the support, tolerance and encouragement given to me by my wife and family, friends and colleagues. Thanks also to the students of Settle High School & Community College.

Order queries: please contact Bookpoint Ltd, 39 Milton Park, Abingdon, Oxon OX14 4TD. Telephone: (44) 01235 400414, Fax: (44) 01235 400454. Lines are open from 9.00 - 6.00, Monday to Saturday, with a 24 hour message answering service. Email address: orders@bookpoint.co.uk

British Library Cataloguing in Publication Data
A catalogue record for this title is available from The British Library

ISBN 0 340 70510 8

First published 1998
Impression number 10 9 8 7 6 5 4 3 2 1
Year   2002 2001 2000 1999 1998

Cover photos supplied by author.

Typeset by Barking Dog Art, Stroud, Gloucestershire.
Designed and illustrated by Barking Dog Art, Stroud Gloucestershire.
Printed in Great Britain for Hodder & Stoughton Educational, a division of Hodder Headline Plc, 338 Euston Road, London NW1 3BH by Redwood Books, Trowbridge, Wiltshire.

Acknowledgements

ABP 6.1, 6.2, 6.3 : Air photo 7.11, 7.32 : Brent Murphy 7.12, 7.32 : Census ONS 1.4, 1.5, 5.1, 6.11 : Craven Herald, 4.4, 4.13, 4.18, 4.22 : David Allen 7.3, 7.8 : Dundee University 2.4, 2.6 : English Estates 5.6 : Environment Agency 1.3, 3.2, 3.6, 3.7, 3.22 : Grattans PLC 5.1, 5.2 : Guardian 5.1 : Holderness Advertiser, 7.1, 7.32 : Holderness Borough Council 7.1, 7.6, 7.7, 7.16, 7.36 : Hull City Council 6.1, 6.9, 6.11, 6.13 : Hull Daily Mail 6.5, 6.8 : John Haines 4.4, 4.9 : National Met Library 2.1, 2.3, 2.5, 2.8 : Ordnance Survey 3.3 : 'Plus' magazine 7.9 : Sam Pearce 4.15 : Simon Ross 3.4 : Sophie Pritchard 3.19 : Bradford Telegraph & Argus 5.12, 5.13 : Wharfe Valley Times 3.13 : Wildgoose Ltd. 4.1 : York Evening Press 2.1, 2.2, 3.1, 3.2 : Yorkshire Dales NP 4.2, 4.3, 4.7, 4.8, 4.19 : Yorkshire Evening Post 4.13, 7.34 : The Sheffield Star 1.1c : A.J.Slaughter 2.7 : all other photos taken by the author.

Bibliography and References not in text

Challenge of the Natural Environment, B. Knapp et al. 1989, Longman, 0582355974
Coastal Erosion - Curriculum resources for Key Stage 4, Humberside Education Services
Decision-Making Geography, N Law and D Smith, 1991, Stanley Thomas, 0748711112
Deprivation and the 1991 census, R Holmes, Geography Review, Jan 1995
Enquiry Skills for GCSE, K Donert, 1990, Heinemann, 0435340115
Fieldwork Techniques and Projects in Geography, B Lenon and P Cleves, 1994, Collins, 0003266435
Geographical Eye, Saving the coast, Yorkshire TV
Hazard Geography, S Ross, 1987, Longman, 0582205506
Kingston upon Hull and Hull Urban Area 1991 Census Atlas c/o John Munson, 1997, Hull City Council
Landform Systems, V Bishop and R Prosser, 1996, Collins, 003266869
Landscape values in the York. Dales, K Willis and G Garrod, 1991, University of Newcastle
National Parks - Yorkshire Dales, 1994, Classroom video
Natural Systems and Human responses, R Prosser, 1992, Nelson, 0174440693
People and Environments, F Slater, 1986, Collins, 0003274020
People in the Physical Landscape, N Punnett, 1987, Macdonald, 0356114708
Question and Answer - coastal erosion, G Corney, Geography Review, Sep 1995
Rebirth of a village, (Saltaire), Telegraph & Argus, March 29th 1996 (see below)
Societies, Choices and Environments, F Slater, Ed., 1991, Collins, 0003274012
Spurn Head, A Day, Geography Review, Feb 1993 (and Withernsea School)
The Human Environment, B Digby, Ed., 1995, Heinemann, 0435352261
The Physical Environment, B Digby, Ed., 1995, Heinemann, 043535227X
Urban Renewal - Hull, N Punnett, Geofile, MGP, Jan 1992
Water in the Landscape, Cambridge Video
Water Resources - process and management, V Bishop and R Prosser, 1996, Collins, 0003266842
Yorkshire Dales National Park 'Visitor' Survey 1992, see below

Contacts

Air Photo, Mablethorpe
Associated British Ports, Port Manager, PO Box No1, Port House, Corporation Road, Hull, North Humberside, HU9 5PQ
Bradford Telegraph and Argus - part of Bradford & District Newspapers, Hall Ings, Bradford
Census marketing, ONS, Segensworth Road, Titchfield, Hampshire, PO15 5RR
Craven Herald, 38 High Street, Skipton - part of Bradford & District Newspapers, Hall Ings, Bradford
Dundee University
Environment Agency (formerly NRA) Regional Office, Rivers House, 21 Park Square South, Leeds, LS1 2QG
Grattans PLC, Anchor House, Ingleby Road, Bradford, West Yorks, BD99 2XG
Holderness Advertiser
Holderness Borough Council, Development Department, Council Offices, Skirlaugh, Hull, North Humberside, HU11 5HN
Hull City Council, Technical Services Department, Kingston House, Bond Street, Kingston upon Hull, HU1 3ER
Hull Daily Mail, PO Box 34, Blundell's Corner, Beverly Road, Hull, HU3 1XS
National Meteorological Library and Archive, Scott Building, Sterling Centre
Ordnance Survey, Romsey Road, Southampton, SO16 4GU
Wildgoose Ltd.
Yorkshire Dales National Park, Education Officer, Colvend, Hebden Road, Grassington, North Yorks, BD23 5LB
Yorkshire Post, Yorkshire Evening Post, Wellington Street, Leeds 1
Yorkshire Evening Press, PO Box 29, 76-86 Walmgate Street, York, YO11 1YN
Yorkshire Water PLC, 2 The Embankment, Sovereign Street, Leeds, LS1 4BG
Further support materials will be available from PJC (educational), Croft House, Austwick, Lancaster, LA2 8BE

Contents

Figure A : a quick guide to identifying your Cartographic, Graphical, Statistical, Decision-Making and other Skills and Techniques

Bi-polar Analysis	7.5	Hydrographs	1.3, 3.2
Census Data Analysis	6.7	Location Quotients	5.1
Chloropleth Mapping	1.4, 6.4, 6.7	Map Interpretation	3.1, 6.1, 7.5
Conflict matrix	4.5, 5.4, 7.4	Photo Analysis	5.3, 7.3, 7.5
Correlation	6.5	Proportional circles	1.4, 5.6
Cost-Benefit Analysis	3.5, 4.5, 4.6, 7.6	Ranking and Weightings	4.4, 7.5
Data Analysis	1.3, 2.4, 3.2, 3.4, 3.6, 4.2-5, 6.2	Satellite images	1.1, 2.2, 4.1
Decision-Making	4.4-6, 5.1, 5.6, 6.2-6, 7.4, 7.6	Significance tests	6.5
		Sketch annotation	3.1, 4.4, 5.3-4, 7.3-5
Deprivation Indicators	6.7	Sketch maps	1.1, 1.4, 3.1, 3.2, 3.6,3.8, 4.1, 6.2, , 6.3 7.2-3
Dispersion diagram	6.4		
Divided bar charts	5.1, 6.4	Spearman's Rank	6.6
Dot distribution maps	1.4	Statistical Analysis	5.6, 6.6
Drawing graphs	4.2, 5.6, 6.1	SWOT Analysis	4.6
Ecological transects	4.3	Synoptic Charts	2.2, 2.3
Environmental Impact Analysis	4.6, 7.5	Systems Diagram	3.5, 4.3, 7.3
Essay Writing	2.3, 3.6, 4.6, 7.7	Transect Diagram	1.2, 2.4, 4.3
Fieldwork	4.2-5, 5.5-6, 7.3-4, 8	Triangular graphs	5.6
Flow diagrams	1.3, 4.2	Values analysis	1.1, 3.3, 3.5, 4.4-6, 6.6, 7.4–5

Figure B : a Quick Guide to identifying your Syllabus Content Topics

People Weather and Climate	Weather and Human Activity	2.1
Landform Management	Physical and Human change in River Systems	1.3, 3.1
	Coastal processes and management	7.1
Natural Hazards	Weather and Floods	2.2
Pollution	River and Estuary management	3.6
Ecosystems	Human impacts	4.3
Recreation Leisure and Tourism		4.1
Urban Change		5.3, 6.4
Resource Management	Water Resources and Drought	3.4
Industrial Change and Economic Activity		5.1, 6.2

Europe in Transition

A Students' Guide to the Teaching and Learning Strategy for the Series

Welcome to a new generation of student-centred regionally based people–environment geography books on the new Europe, and the first such series for 20 years. As we approach the millennium, we are seeing a new and dynamic Europe that is changing in response to socio-economic and political factors and the challenge of a changing physical environment. The series is designed to assist you with your AS-level, A-level and first year undergraduate studies by encouraging you not only to read and make your notes on up-to-date material, but also to develop other key study skills and enhance your tool box of geographical techniques.

The series will eventually include regions from North and South, East and West. It will cover core and peripheral areas, well-known and lesser-known geographical case studies, and include regions of transitional change and contrastingly those experiencing more rapid changes.

We aim to make every volume both very accessible and yet challenging, and hope you will enjoy this approach and find the content stimulating. The series has been designed to be used in four ways:

1) *As a foundation book for a regional study.* This may be: (a) an extensive course; or (b) a more limited range of sections or case studies might be used to form a 2–3 week transition/ introduction to a new course, e.g. for London Syll B A-level, a student-centred skills-based introductory/transitional unit could be produced using 4–5 double-page spreads. The exact sections would depend on the options taken by the centre/ student and the exact skills and techniques that need to be covered. Figure A and B on page (v) allow you to rapidly identify the content topics and geographical techniques you may wish to include. There is extensive cross-referencing of sections to allow you to follow a theme through this book.

For a more extensive course we would suggest that students work through the material chapter by chapter, building up a more detailed understanding of general concepts and processes with comprehensive case studies. In addition, acquiring a wide range of skills and geographical techniques.

2) *To cover specific content-based sections of courses.* Use page (iv) and page (v) to rapidly identify relevant case study sections, e.g. Regional Disparities, Ecosystems or Recreation.

3) *You may wish to learn about a particular geographical technique.* Use Fig. A on page (v) to identify a relevant task that will help you to practise and master this skill area, e.g. Cost Benefit Analysis or Choropleth mapping.

4) *As an introduction or follow-up to a residential field-course or study visit.* There are numerous ideas for fieldwork throughout the book, and a number of field study centres are to be found within the Yorkshire region.

Steve Frampton, series editor

The Yorkshire Region

People–environment issues in a changing region

The Yorkshire Region provides up-to-date information on a region which has long been studied by geographers. The region contains a variety of landforms, ecosystems and rural and urban communities which have changed considerably over the last thirty years. This text will introduce students to the people–environment issues created by this change and highlight the need for effective management and decision-making. As the introductory chapter will show, the geography of the region is varied, yet retains an identity of its own.

An enquiry approach to learning is built into each chapter with task boxes, which allow further investigations of case studies or key issues. A range of geographical techniques are introduced and students are encouraged to develop skills through the use of 'Technique Panels'. A unique feature is the careful integration of chapters which have been designed to communicate key aspects of the changing geography of the region. The variety of teaching and learning styles will add depth to students' studies. For this reason, the text can be used as a foundation book designed to give regional context to geographical study. It can also be used by students dipping into chapters for case study information for key areas of the new Geography AS and A-level syllabuses.

The penultimate chapter is written as an open learning assignment to allow students to use the resources provided along with the skills they have already acquired to plan their own geographical enquiry. The last chapter looks at and guides students towards those issues that will form part of the region's future.

I hope that this text gives you a better understanding of the region, as well as of Geography, and that you may wish to visit the region to increase your knowledge through fieldwork or research issues more fully using the large range of secondary sources available.

As you work through this book is would be useful to have handy a good atlas, or better still to use a copy of the Ordnance Survey Routemaster sheet No. 5, Northern England.

The case studies used in this book do offer a fair balance of issues and places with the region, whilst inevitably they also reflect my own interests and experiences. I am also acutely conscious of those examples which I have not found room to include in these pages. Might I especially apologise to those expecting chapters on the Lower Don valley, the North York Moors, on the impacts of modern agriculture, and the regional importance of Leeds. All alas remain 'on the cutting-room floor'.

Bob Hordern, author

1 INTRODUCTION

Key Ideas and Concepts
- Regional images
- Geology and relief
- Geology and scenery
- Land use and scenery
- Drainage patterns
- Population and settlements
- Economic development
- Communications network

General Skills
- Photograph analysis
- Map analysis
- Map annotation
- Graphical analysis
- Poster design

Geographical Techniques
- Satellite images
- Sketch maps
- Transect diagrams
- Flow diagrams
- Choropleth mapping
- Dot distribution map
- Proportional symbols

1.1 The region and its images

Yorkshire with its three 'ridings' was once the largest county in England and Wales, covering an area of over 15 000 km². It is not surprising therefore that even in its modern, smaller version it shows great variety – from the lonely moorlands on the Pennine hills to the crowded beaches of the east coast – from the traditional farming villages of the Vale of York to the modern metropolitan cities of West and South Yorkshire. The photographs on this page and the suite of maps that follow try to paint a portrait of this **regional identity and variety**.

Fig 1.1d

Upland scenery for quiet recreation as seen here in the North York Moors. (See the Dales scenery in Fig. 4.1.)

Fig 1.1a

Woollen mills are the enduring image that many people still have of Yorkshire, as seen here at Saltaire, near Bradford. (See the photo in Fig. 5.1.)

Fig 1.1b

Business sites available in most cities, as seen here in Bradford. (See the results in Fig. 5.9.)

Fig 1.1e *Agriculture still occupies much of the rural areas as seen here in North Yorkshire.*

Fig 1.1c

Modern regional shopping provision is increasing as seen here at Meadowhall, Sheffield. (See the CBD response in Fig. 6.5)

TASK BOX

The region and its images:

Using these resources:
1. Comment on the images suggested by the photographs - consider ideas such as identity, variety, positive and negative.

2. Compare the satellite image (inside front cover) with the series of maps which follow in this chapter and try to identify any features you see:
    (a) which sorts of features stand out most and why is this so?
    (b) what are the advantages and disadvantages of satellite images and topographic maps?

1.2 Relief and geology

The Yorkshire region has relatively clear boundaries that are closely linked to the relief of the area, the underlying geology, and the drainage pattern of the Humber basin. Within the region this varied relief has helped to create a number of sub-regions, each with their own distinct scenery. The rocks are in much evidence, most noticeably in the upland areas of the Yorkshire Dales (see Figure 4.1) and the North York Moors (see previous section). It is partly due to this that these two areas have been designated as National Parks. In general, the older Carboniferous rocks, with their greater resistance to erosion, form the higher ground of the Pennines, whilst the younger less consolidated rocks have produced the lowland plains of the east. In between these extremes are the narrow dales valleys and wide lowlands of the Ouse. This pattern is further punctuated in the east by the escarpments that cross the region, emphasising the north–south structure. As well as the present drainage pattern (see section 1.3), there has been the effect of glaciation (see inset 2) when ice entered the region and also contributed to the shape of the present day landscape. In the chapter that follows, relief will emerge as an important influence on the geography of the Yorkshire region.

TASK BOX

The relief and geology:

1. Use these resources to draw a large sketch map of the region and mark on it the seven sub-regions shown on inset 1. Pennines, Yorkshire Coalfield, North York Moors, Vale of Picking, Yorkshire Wolds and Holderness.

2. Use insets 2 and 3, the photos in sections 1.1 and those referred to in the text to annotate the map with brief comment about relief, geology and scenery.

3. Use the cross-section below and information from section 1.5 to construct a *transect diagram* that links relief and geology with scenery and land use (see section 2.4 for an example of how to use this technique).

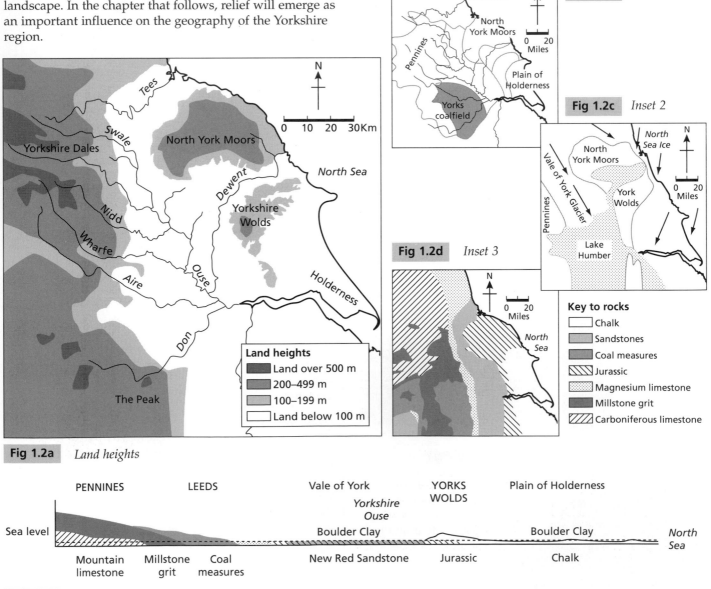

Fig 1.2b   *Inset 1*

Fig 1.2c   *Inset 2*

Fig 1.2d   *Inset 3*

Key to rocks

- ☐ Chalk
- ▨ Sandstones
- ▨ Coal measures
- ▧ Jurassic
- ▨ Magnesium limestone
- ▨ Millstone grit
- ▨ Carboniferous limestone

Fig 1.2a   *Land heights*

Land heights
- Land over 500 m
- 200–499 m
- 100–199 m
- Land below 100 m

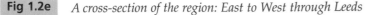

Fig 1.2e   *A cross-section of the region: East to West through Leeds*

PENNINES   LEEDS   Vale of York   YORKS WOLDS   Plain of Holderness

Yorkshire Ouse

Sea level   Boulder Clay   Boulder Clay   North Sea

Mountain limestone   Millstone grit   Coal measures   New Red Sandstone   Jurassic   Chalk

1.3 Drainage pattern

The Humber basin has the largest catchment area of any estuary in the UK. It receives most of its run-off from the Ouse and Trent river systems – a fifth of the area of England. Most of the Yorkshire rivers have their origins in the Pennine hills where the varied Carboniferous rocks determine the 'hardness' of the water. The pattern of drainage also results from this underlying geology, through the effects of glaciation have been considerable. Hydrological issues in the upper courses of these rivers centre round water storage, whilst the more complex matters of flood control, water abstraction and pollution dominate their lower courses.

Each of these graphs shows three aspects of discharge.
1 – the mean decade flow 1985–95
2 – the flow in 1995
3 – the mean monthly flow in cumecs

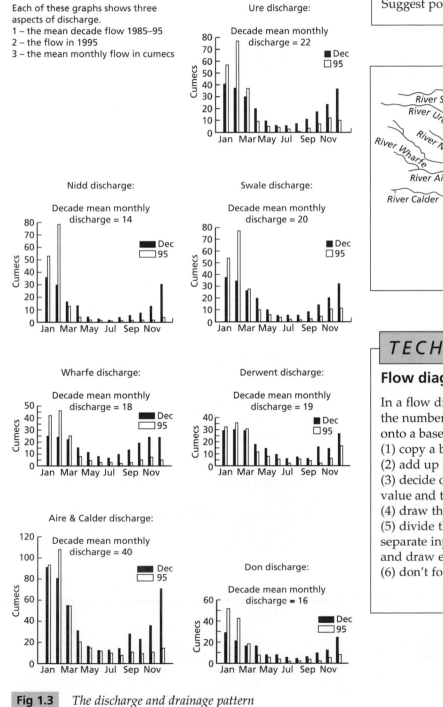

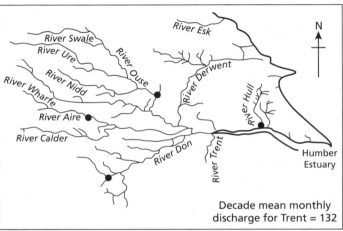

Decade mean monthly discharge for Trent = 132

Fig 1.3   *The discharge and drainage pattern*

TECHNIQUES PANEL

Flow diagrams

In a flow diagram, the thickness of the arrows represents the number or amount involved. They may be drawn onto a base map
(1) copy a base map
(2) add up data to get total (e.g. 22+14+20 etc)
(3) decide on a suitable scale that covers both the smallest value and the total
(4) draw the total flow first
(5) divide this up into its separate inputs (or outputs) and draw each on the map
(6) don't forget a key

scale 1mm = 10 cumes

1.4 Population and settlement

When publishing data about social and economic changes in the UK, the government uses standard statistical regions. The standard region used in this book is Yorkshire and Humberside, and whilst other political boundaries may change, as was seen in 1996 for Hull and Lincolnshire, it seems likely that these large statistical regions will remain.

Some of this region remains relatively lightly populated compared with other parts of the country, most notably in rural North Yorkshire. However, in the metropolitan counties of West and South Yorkshire, population density is much greater. Sheffield is the single largest settlement in the region and it has become an important service centre following the decline of its steel-making industry.

The county of Humberside has, since 1996, been divided into the separate local government areas of East Yorkshire, the city of Hull and North Lincolnshire.

	North Yorkshire	*West Yorkshire*	*UK overall*
Population changes (%) 1981–1992	+7	+1	+3
Birth rate (per 1000)	11	14	13
Young people (%)	18	21	30
Death rate (per 1000)	11	10	11
Old people (%)	20	17	20
Ethnic minority (%)	<1	>7	5.5
West Yorkshire pop.		2 013 693	
South Yorkshire pop.		1 262 630	
North Yorkshire pop.		702 661	
Humberside pop.		858 040	

Fig 1.4a   *Population fact file*

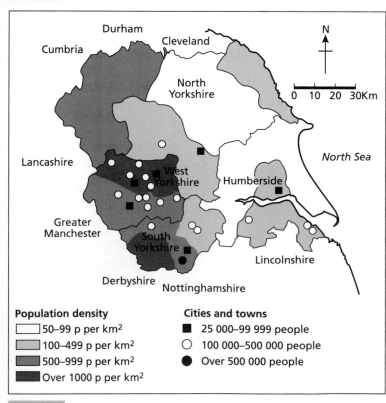

Fig 1.4b   *Population density*

Population density
- ☐ 50–99 p per km²
- ☐ 100–499 p per km²
- ☐ 500–999 p per km²
- ☐ Over 1000 p per km²

Cities and towns
- ■ 25 000–99 999 people
- ○ 100 000–500 000 people
- ● Over 500 000 people

TECHNIQUES PANEL

Dot distribution maps:

In these maps, dots are placed evenly within an area to represent the totals to be plotted, e.g. one dot may represent perhaps 100 000 people.

(1) copy a base map

(2) decide on a scale that copes with the lowest and the highest values to be used

(3) work out the number of dots needed and arrange these evenly within the area involved

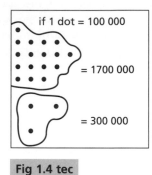

Fig 1.4 tec

(4) complete each area in turn, keeping the dots evenly spaced and the same size

TASK BOX

Population and settlement:

1. Draw a sketch map of the region to show the four countries of Humberside, and North, South and West Yorkshire. Annotate each to highlight their differing population densities and the urban centres involved.

2. Use the fact-file to show how the population characteristics of Yorkshire's 'shire' county (North) differ from its metropolitan county (West).

3. Compare this *choropleth* map of population density (Figure 1.4b) with the map of land use in section 1.5 which follows. Briefly give reasons for any relationships you see.

4. Use the total population data to produce a *dot distribution map* of Yorkshire's counties (see box).

5. Use these maps and an A-level textbook to research the techniques of choropleth mapping (see section 6.4), *proportional symbols* (see section 5.6) and dot distribution maps. Draw up a table to compare the situations in which you would use them, and their advantages and their disadvantages.

1.5 Economic development and transport

Agriculture varies a good deal across the Yorkshire region and this relates to the physical geography of the area its climate, relief and soils as well as the economic factors – the role of markets and farm subsidies. The larger urban centres and their immediate surroundings have traditionally provided the resources and work force for the region's manufacturing industries, however there has been much diversification as the region now has numerous footloose industries (see sections 5.1 and 5.2). Hull, the region's main port, has also seen considerable change (see section 6.3). Tourism, inland rather than on the coast (see section 4.2), continues to expand rapidly, popularised by television media, giving the Yorkshire region a strong regional identity. As part of its response to these changes, the region has developed its transport network, particularly its motorways.

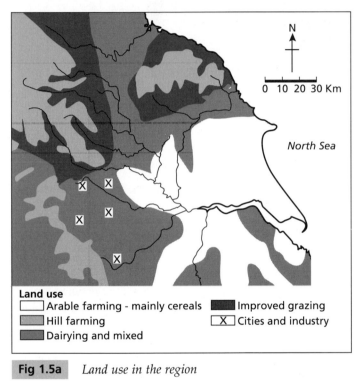

Land use
☐ Arable farming - mainly cereals	■ Improved grazing
▨ Hill farming	☒ Cities and industry
▨ Dairying and mixed	

Fig 1.5a   *Land use in the region*

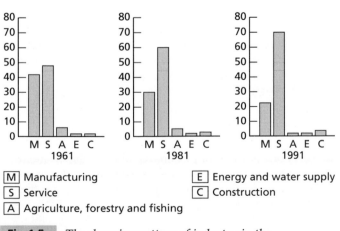

M	Manufacturing
S	Service
A	Agriculture, forestry and fishing
E	Energy and water supply
C	Construction

Fig 1.5c   *The changing pattern of industry in the Yorkshire region*

We're waiting to welcome you

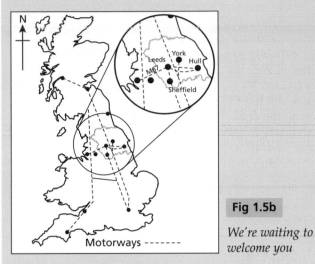

Fig 1.5b

We're waiting to welcome you

Wide range of grants available
Urban (see section 6.4 on 'economy')
Rural (see section 4.6 on funding)

Growing motorway, rail and air traffic
Network within and beyond the region

Skilled, adaptable workforce
Competitive pricing and a wide choice
Of Greenfield and inner city sites (see section 5.2)

Attractively price housing at all levels
Metro-centre type shopping (see section 1.1)
Leisure and recreation facilities from sports venues to
National Parks to coastal resorts (see sections 1.1, 4.4 and Chapter 7)

TASK BOX

Economic development and transport

1. Briefly describe the pattern of rural land use across the region in relation to relief and geology (see section 1.2). Suggest what factors might have influenced the location of cities and heavy industry?

2. Describe and explain the changing pattern of industry shown in Figure 1.5c. Draw up a list of possible advantages and disadvantages of the region for new industry.

4. Use Figure 1.5b, photos from section 1.1, and ideas from section 5 to design a leaflet or poster to attract footloose industries to the Yorkshire region. Justify your design.

2 PEOPLE AND WEATHER

Key Ideas and Concepts
- Weather and climate
- Patterns of weather
- Winter depressions
- A summer anticyclone
- The impact of weather on people

General Skills
- Photograph analysis
- Data analysis
- Mapping skills
- Annotated diagrams
- Values analysis

Geographical Techniques
- Synoptic charts
- Satellite images
- Transect diagram

2.1 Weather and climate

Weather and climate have a combined impact upon people's daily lives and activities. Whilst on one hand the nature of the climate has long term effects upon a region's economic activities, such as agriculture and tourism, the day-to-day and seasonal variations of the weather can have more localised, short term effects on farming, business, health, leisure and transport.

Extreme meteorological events such as winter snow, spring floods or summer drought focus our attention on the management problems we sometimes face.

Fig 2.1

The effects of the winter weather across Yorkshire

2.2 Winter weather

As 1981 drew to a close and the New Year of 1982 began, the weather condition at that time focused our attention upon the vagaries of our UK weather and the challenges we face. In the Yorkshire region in particular, the effects were considerable both before and after the Christmas period. The resources in sections 2.2 and 3.1 will outline both the causes and the socio-economic effects involved.

Chaos as 4ft drifts hit Yorkshire villages

North Yorkshire was in chaos today after a blizzard left villages isolated and minor roads blocked. Up to six inches of snow fell last night and gale-force winds caused serious drifts. A motorist died in his snowbound car on the A59 near Skipton. In all, 19 people were rescued from 10 vehicles.

Earlier today, trains in the Leeds area came to a standstill. The snow followed the coldest night of the year. The temperature at Upper Poppleton was 18 F (−4 C). In York, the Royal Station Hotel's 128 rooms were all full as travellers waited for the weather to improve. The snow hit schools in North Yorkshire. 1400 people in Whitby were without electricity for three hours last night.

A helicopter from RAF Linton flew a Malton woman to hospital for urgent kidney treatment as roads over the Wolds were impassable. There were reportedly falls of twelve inches on high ground. At the Smedley-HP factory at Barlby, three coaches failed to turn up to bring workers in. In York, the River Ouse is frozen over. No mail arrived in the city today. An AA spokesman warned motorists who must travel to "take blankets, chocolates and a shovel in case you get caught in a snow storm".

York Evening Press, 14 December 1981

A wider view of Britain

11 December:
Five people were killed when one train ploughed into the back of another in a blinding snowstorm at Beaconsfield, near London.

12 December:
In London where driving snow made Big Ben's clock run slow, the Weather Centre blamed a high pressure system over Greenland for the strong Arctic winds.

13 December:
Thousands of passengers at Heathrow are sleeping rough in Terminal Three as snow piles six inches deep on the runways. Freezing fog is also a problem. Glasgow airport reported its coldest December on record with temperatures of 9 F (−13 C) overnight.

Fig 2.2   *The effects of the winter weather across Britain*

TASK BOX

Winter weather

Look at the resources in sections 2.2 and 3.1.
1. Describe the nature and pattern of the weather.

2. Select one of the synoptic charts and its related satellite image. On an outline map of western Europe, sketch in the changing features of the depression and explain the processes at work.

3. Outline the background to the two weather situations using the notes on page 7. Why was the weather different?

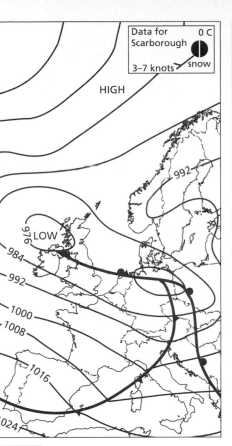

Fig 2.3 *Synoptic chart: 12 noon, 14 December 1981*

Forecast - 6am to midnight (December 14th 1981)

A LOW will move away eastwards as a new LOW approaches western Scotland.

Yorkshire - Sleet or snow showers, bright intervals, wind variable, becoming westerly. Maximum temperature 1° to 3°C.

London - Showers of rain or sleet, sunny, wind westerly, strong to moderate. Maximum temperature 5° to 7°C.

Outlook for next few days - Staying cold with wintry showers in all areas.

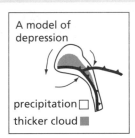

Summary - Low pressure, winds blow anticlockwise, rising air brings cloud, precipitation occurs along fronts, unsettled weather, general movement is west to east.

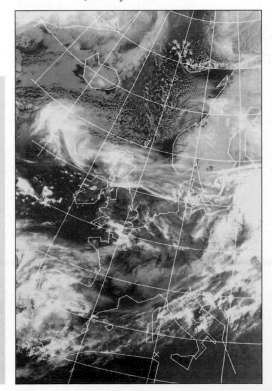

Fig 2.4 *Satellite image: 2 pm, 14 December 1981*

Fig 2.5 *Synoptic chart: 12 noon, 4 January 1982*

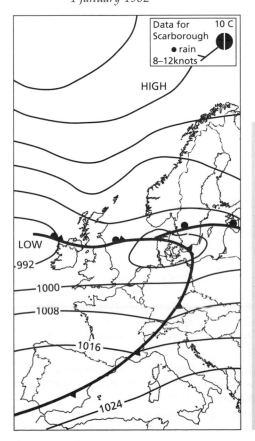

Key
Fronts–warm
Cold
Occluded
Isobars showing air pressure
———1032———

Fig 2.6 *Satellite image: 1.30 pm, 4 January 1982*

Forecast - 6am to midnight (January 4th 1982)

Troughs of LOW pressure will move slowly eastwards across northern and central Britain.

Yorkshire - Rain turning to snow later, wind becoming easterly, moderate to fresh. Maximum temperature 7° to 9°C.

London - Showers, outbreaks of rain, sunny intervals, wind SW, fresh locally strong. Maximum temperature 9° to 11°C.

Outlook for tomorrow and Wednesday. Bright and cold in all northern areas.

2.3 Summer weather

As the summer of 1995 went on, most of the UK remained under the influence of anticyclonic conditions and our weather took on a continental pattern of clear skies, high temperatures and no rain. These drought conditions and the problems they brought were to last well into the autumn and become, in the eyes of the media, very much associated with the West Yorkshire region. See section 3.4.

TASK BOX

Summer weather

Look at the resources in sections 2.3 and 3.4.
1. Describe the effects this weather had on the people of West Yorkshire.

2. Explain why some groups of people might actually have 'gained' from this weather?

3. Explain the meteorological situation that led to these weather conditions.

Fig 2.7

Bank holiday in Scarborough

Figure 2.9: Meteorological background

Unstable polar and tropical air masses crossing the Atlantic bring rain-bearing winds, which are forced to rise as they cross the Pennine hills. Depressions, often occurring in groups, are a common feature of this prevailing westerly maritime air flow.

The combined effect of this relief and frontal rainfall produces high levels of precipitation in the upland areas of the western Dales. In contrast to this, the lowland areas to the west generally experience drier conditions, as a result of what is called the 'rain shadow' effect. In the west, temperatures are influenced greatly by altitude. The east generally records more hours of sunshine in the summer, though 'frets' or sea fogs can affect holidays in the east coast resorts.

In winter, when the pressure is high and stable Arctic or continental airmasses prevail, the Vale of York and the cross-Pennine motorway routes are prone to fog. Very cold and snowy weather can seriously disrupt life and business throughout the region. Spring rain and sudden thaws often lead to flooding in central lowland areas.

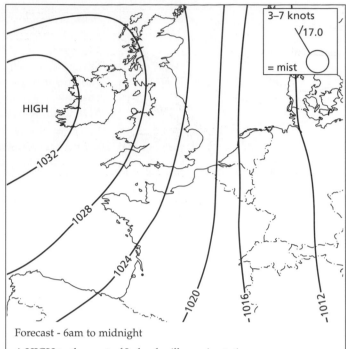

Forecast - 6am to midnight

A HIGH to the west of Ireland will remain stationary.
England and Wales - Dry, with bright sunshine, calm. Maximum temperature 28°–30°C.
Outlook for the next few days - Staying hot in all areas.

Key
Isobars showing air pressure 1024.

Fig 2.8   *Synoptic chart: 12 noon, 28 August 1995*

Summary - High pressure, light winds blow clockwise, sinking air so little cloud, fine settled weather in summer. Clear skies mean frost and fog in winter. Slow moving and cover a large area.

TASK BOX

Weather and climate: a summary

1. Copy and complete the cross-section of the transect diagram. Complete and annotate it using the climate data provided and the processes outlined in Figure 2.12.

2. Write a brief summary which shows the effects of relief on the region's climate.

3. Identify which ideas, facts and diagrams from Chapters 2 and 3 you would use to answer these questions:
    (a) outline the causes of seasonal variation in the weather and climate of the Yorkshire region.
    (b) show how seasonal variations can have short term impacts on people's lives.

4. Using Figure 2.11,
    (a) describe the sequence of weather experienced during the passage of a depression west to east through the region.
    (b) What hazards and effects might it cause?

2.4 Summary

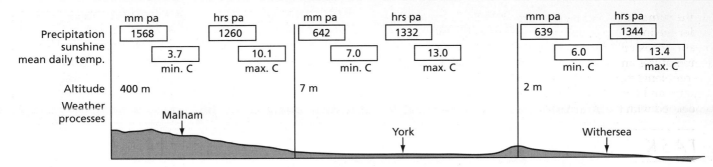

Precipitation sunshine mean daily temp.	mm pa **1568** **3.7** min. C	hrs pa **1260** **10.1** max. C	mm pa **642** **7.0** min. C	hrs pa **1332** **13.0** max. C	mm pa **639** **6.0** min. C	hrs pa **1344** **13.4** max. C
Altitude	400 m		7 m		2 m	

Weather processes

Malham   York   Withersea

Fig 2.10   *The influences of climate and weather across the region*

Relief	Pennine hills and Yorkshire Dales	Vale of York/Yorkshire Wolds	Plain of Holderness	North Sea
Landforms	Rainwater dissolves limestone	River floodplain/Chalk escarpment	Boulder clay lowland	
Water problems and water resources	Heavy winter rain can produce local flooding, e.g. Skipton. Reservoirs built in narrow glaciated valleys, e.g. Nidderdale	Spring floods where rivers meet, e.g. York and Cawood. Water abstracted from rivers or from aquifers, e.g. Ouse	Storms and NE winds erode coast surges flood estuary lowlands.	
Farming	Heavy snow can put livestock at risk on hill farms, e.g. early lambs. Low winter sunshine record limits crop choice, e.g. silage not hay.	Drier climate allows arable, oil seed rape and barley. Longer growing season - enables crop diversity.		
Leisure problems and tourism resources	Relatively short holiday season. High runoff damages footpaths. Scenery of fast-flowing rivers, e.g. Ingleton 'Waterfalls' walk.			
Travel and transport	Winter snow can block main roads, e.g. A59 Skipton to Harrogate. Winrer fog brings accidents, e.g. M62 section near Huddersfield.			
Other	Increase in wind turbine planning applications, e.g. Flight Hill.			

TECHNIQUES PANEL

Transect diagrams

Transects are a means of sampling an area to discover its geographical characteristics, and they are usually based upon a line or belt along which data is collected. The results are then shown on a transect diagram.

1. Select a suitable transect line.
2. Draw a scale cross-section along this line.
3. Label it to show the changing characteristics.
4. Underneath, arrange the information collected into separate rows. The resulting matrix can be used to show the related causes, consequences or management.

A cross-section through a typical depression
Direction of movement of system

TROPOPAUSE

Height (m)

Ci Cs   Ci

Warm air   Cs

Cold air   As   Cold air

Cu   Ns

St   Cu   Sc

10 000

5000

0

2000   1500   1000   500   0
Rain   Rain
Kilometres

Many depressions are much less active and slower-moving

Ci Cirrus
Cs Cirrostratus   Sc Stratocumulus   As Altostratus
Ns Nimbostratus   Cu Cumulus   St Stratus

Fig 2.11   *A cross section through a depression*

Moist air rises
cooled by expansion
water vapour condenses
clouds and rain form

Air descends
warmed by compression
little evaporation
clear skies and little rain

direction of movement

SEA   MOUNTAINS   RAIN SHADOW AREA

Fig 2.12   *A model of relief (orographic) rainfall*

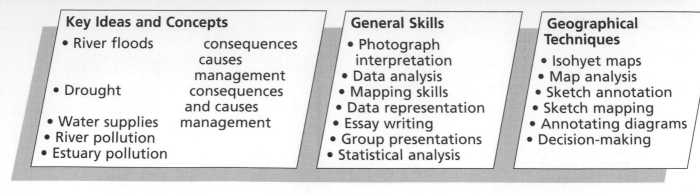

Key Ideas and Concepts
- River floods   consequences
              causes
              management
- Drought   consequences
              and causes
- Water supplies   management
- River pollution
- Estuary pollution

General Skills
- Photograph interpretation
- Data analysis
- Mapping skills
- Data representation
- Essay writing
- Group presentations
- Statistical analysis

Geographical Techniques
- Isohyet maps
- Map analysis
- Sketch annotation
- Sketch mapping
- Annotating diagrams
- Decision-making

3.1 River floods: the consequences

Fig 3.1   *River floods looking downstream towards the bridge at Cawood*

Flooding in large catchments like those that drain the Yorkshire region into the Humber is inevitable. In fact, whilst it may be sensible to try to prevent flooding to protect homes and large urban areas, allowing rivers to spill on to the so-called 'washland' in their upper courses does prevent more serious flooding downstream. The floodplain of the river Ouse near York is one such area. As we saw in Chapter 2, the weather at the end of 1981 and in the first few days of 1982, triggered the worst floods in that area since the spring of 1947.

City braced as Ouse nears crisis

York today braced itself for the worst flooding since 1978, when 600 homes were flooded.

Emergency services stood by as the Ouse rose to danger level. The river, swollen by melting snow and heavy rain, rose throughout the day. The critical time was expected to be between 6pm and 10pm when the level was predicted to reach 15ft 10in (4.8 m).

Throughout the city people living in low-lying areas held their breath. Flood defences, built since the last major disaster in 1978 seemed to be holding back the water.

An emergency flood control centre was set up at York police station HQ in Fulford Road. A second flood control centre has been set up at Selby civic centre. A police spokesman said the Ouse had topped its banks at Cawood. Elsewhere, roads were closed for a time by flood water from the Aire. The Wharfe at Tadcaster is 10ft (3 m) above normal and the Ure has burst its banks at Boroughbridge.

Yorkshire Evening Press Jan 4th 1982

Selby comes 'within inches of disaster'

Selby was within inches of disaster when the level of the Ouse started dropping last night.

About 150 homes were flooded but a further 850 were threatened. Today it was hoped to start pumping some of the water back into the river.

Rivers chiefs said that the main reason for Selby's great escape was the sudden cold snap which slowed the rate at which water entered rivers in the county.

Yesterday, in addition to food by boat to farms cut off by flood water, troops took heaters to places where mopping-up could begin.

Buses in York were today running normally, though overnight freezing was a problem. Telephones were being reconnected in parts of York and Boroughbridge. Schools hit by the floods were struggling to get back to normal.

Insurance companies were beginning to receive claims for damage which is estimated at millions of pounds. York's major house insurance firm today offered cash advances to help flood victims make their homes habitable again.

Yorkshire Evening Press Jan 7th 1982

Fig 3.2   *Changing press reports*

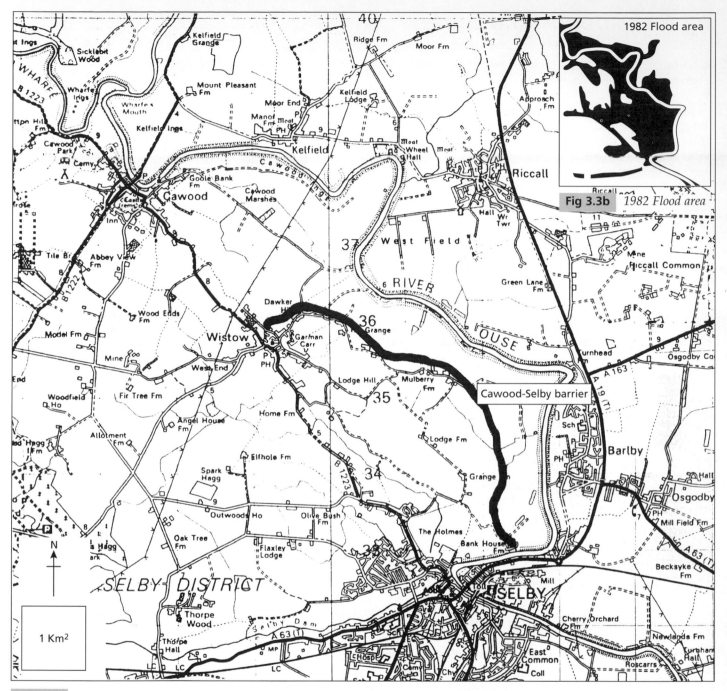

Fig 3.3b *1982 Flood area*

Fig 3.3a   *Ordnance Survey map of the River Ouse below Cawood*

'At Cawood the river overflowed the defences under construction and inundated 90 properties in the village. Floodwater overflowed in Kelfield Ings, severing the Cawood to York road. Four properties in Kelfield village were flooded. Overflow into Cawood marshes spread downstream into the Wistow Lordship and the northern outskirts of Selby, inundating an area of 1,370 hectares, with about 15 million cubic metres of floodwater up to a maximum depth of 2.9 metres. The village of Wistow was isolated with 12 properties flooded together with farmhouses in Wistow Lordship. In Bondgate and the northern areas of Selby, 118 houses suffered flooding to depths of up to 1 metre. Industrial premises were also affected.

Source: Yorkshire Water Authority extract

Fig 3.4   *The area which flooded in 1982*

TASK BOX

The consequences of flooding

1. Show how both the content and message of the two reports in Figure 3.2 changed.

2. Use the OS map extract and the notes from the Yorkshire Water Authority to trace the area likely to have been flooded. There is an inset map to help you. Annotate your map to show river features and the effects on land uses, roads, villages, etc.

3. Draw and annotate a sketch based on Figure 3.1, to show the physical and social consequences of flooding.

xplain wh   od was an obvious flood location.

3.2 River floods: the causes

Flooding occurs when the volume of water in a river is too great for the channel to contain it.

As we saw in Chapter 2, the arrival of a depression in the first few days of 1982, and the resulting increases in air temperature and the onset of yet more rainfall, was a major cause of the flooding that followed. However, it is important to realise that this is only the input into the hydrological system. In a catchment like the Ouse, the response of tributary streams to rainfall or snowmelt will vary in both amount and timing, depending on their varied hydrological characteristics. Where a number of streams meet, such as at York, the differing pulses of discharge can produce combined effects that result in water levels very much higher than normal.

The causes of flooding are also human in origin and directly relate to people's use of the land within the catchment. Some of these are listed opposite, but perhaps the two most significant impacts result from deforestation and urbanisation, both of which dramatically increase surface runoff.

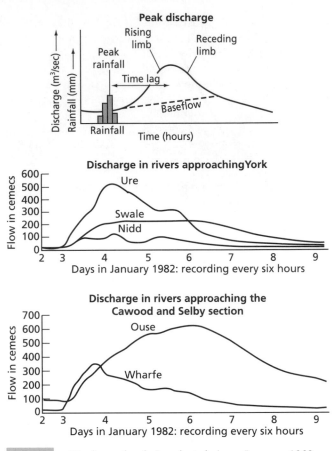

Fig 3.5

Floods in York, January 1982

Figure 3.6: Factors likely to cause or increase flood risk:
- well-developed meanders
- river channels made narrower in urban areas
- erosion of peat by walkers and overgrazing
- arrival of depression with marked warm front
- improvement (gripping) of upland pasture
- high spring tides in lower course
- land only a few metres above sea level
- urban (impermeable) surfaces increase run-off
- floodplain is particularly flat and wide
- confluence of three rivers are very close together
- frozen ground and previous snowfall
- settlements are a bridging or confluence points
- floodwater can back up into tributaries
- some railway embankments run across valleys
- drainage of marshland for arable crops
- removal of woodland from upper catchments
- extensive use of floodplains for livestock rearing
- long profile (gradient) or river is very gentle

Fig 3.7 *Discharge levels in selected rivers January 1982*

TASK BOX

The causes of flooding

Before you begin this task refer back to the data and maps of the relief and drainage of the Humber basin in Chapter 1, and the weather information for January 1982 in Chapter 2. Carefully read the text and using the resources on this page:

1. Classify the list of factors shown in Figure 3.6 into three groups: weather conditions, other natural characteristics, and people's use of the land.

2. Make a large (A4) copy of the Ouse drainage basin: choose up to ten of these factors and suggest places where they might apply (the management resources opposite will help you) - annotate your map naming both the location and the factor involved.

3. Explain how these factors can cause or increase the risk of flooding, referring to your examples.

4. Analyse the two hydrographs showing the discharge of rivers upstream and downstream of York in the first few days of January 1982.
(a) compare the patterns of discharge in the tributaries.
(b) suggest which factors may have caused their individual responses to be different.

3.3 River floods: management

Flood management obviously involves tackling the causes listed in the last section, but successful management means choosing the most appropriate option, based perhaps on environmental, economic and social criteria. The options can be classified in the same way as coastlines, i.e. behavioural and physical (see Chapter 7). An alternative is to group responses as adjustments, abatement and protection (see below). Decisions are ultimately based upon two key ideas: some sort of cost-benefit analysis, and the estimated flood recurrence interval.

Responses likely to prevent or decrease flood risk.
These can be classified as:

Adjustment (this is in the floodplain)
Doing nothing; emergency action; floodproofing of building; land use regulation and zoning; finance and insurance.

Abatement (this is in the catchment)
Afforestation; other vegetational changes; changing agricultural practices; reservoirs; control in urban areas; management of snow-melt areas.

Protection (this is action along the channel)
Building of walls and embankments; detention basins; channel improvement; diversion schemes; barrages and flood barriers.

Fig 3.8   *Responses to the flood hazard*

TASK BOX

The management of flooding

1. Outline the range of management options used by the authorities in the York area.

2. Label your earlier map tracing to show the purpose and extent of the Cawood-Selby Barrier.

3. Evaluate the design of schemes chosen to protect the Ouse floodplain both in York and downstream, on economic, social and environmental grounds.

4. Research other options and try to explain why they may have been avoided in this catchment?

Fig 3.9   *The Foss Barrier. What does it do?*

Figure 3.10: Flood management schemes in the Ouse catchment

Range of responses in the Ouse basin
To adjust to flooding. York has a hi-tech emergency warning system co-ordinated by the police, and the Environment Agency. As an historic centre, it insures and floodproofs its buildings and treasures.

In the catchment area, the Yorkshire Dales National Park has programmes of reforestation in Swaledale and upper Wharfdale, and is working with farmers to 'set aside' land in Wensleydale. Yorkshire Water has large reservoir interests in the upper reaches of the rivers Nidd, Washburn and Wharfe.

Flood defences within York (see Figure 3.9)
Flood defence in the city has cost £7 million.

Walls, floodgates and earth banks have been built along the sides of the Ouse to prevent overflow and protect sewers. The York Water Works Co. has secured its drinking water plant at Acomb Landing from flooding, and Holgate Beck has been rechannelled and diverted south. Clifton Ings takes floodwater.

The most impressive scheme is however the Foss Barrier. In flood conditions, the 16.5 tonne turnover liftgate prevents water from the Ouse backing up into the Foss Beck tributary, yet still enables Foss water to be pumped uphill into the Ouse.

The Cawood-Selby Barrier (see Figure 3.3)
South of York the meanders and natural levees of the Ouse have been built up to increase the cross-section of the channel and form a flood protection barrier from Wharfe's Mouth (GR 574390) to Selby.
The designers had to allow for:
- the effects of mining subsidence (the Selby coalfield spine roads run beneath the area)
- a 50 year scheme life
- washland flood provision
- preserving current farming practice
- flood pulse waves of up to 2 m
- the effects of spring tides
The main bank is 5.5 km long and its height was built to be 8 m above sea level. Completed by 1985, the cost was £3.25 million whilst maintenance and other operations costs are currently £2500 p.a.

Given that the scheme was not designed to prevent all flooding, but to offer protection to floodplain property and activities, so far it is a success, socially, operationally and environmentally.

It is also within the original benefit/cost ratio of 5:4 (1.25). The real test would be a 1982-style event coinciding with a high tide.

3.4 Drought in West Yorkshire - the consequences and causes

The summer of 1995 was the driest since records began. Reservoir stocks decreased rapidly with little rain, hot sun, and high demand - and West Yorkshire reservoirs were the worst affected of all. Significantly, this area is hilly, has few aquifers, and a large urban population. This brought the possibility of standpipes and rota cuts closer as first Bradford, and then Leeds, and most seriously, Calderdale began to literally run out of water. However, despite enormous criticism from the media, ranging from the high salaries of its boardroom to a rumoured 25 percent leakage rate from pipes, Yorkshire Water PLC managed to cope using hosepipe bans, additional pipelines and pumping stations, and an expensive tankering operation.

Fig 3.11   *Thurscross reservoir near Harrogate: tourists stroll along the streets of what was West End village, flooded 30 years ago for Leeds water supplies.*

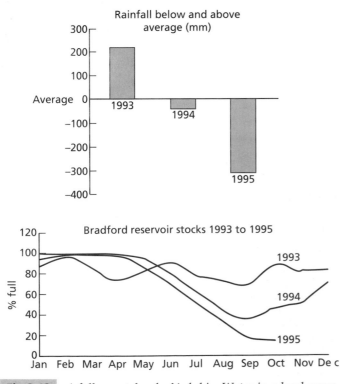

Rainfall below and above average (mm)

Bradford reservoir stocks 1993 to 1995

Fig 3.13   *A full page taken by Yorkshire Water in a local paper, the Wharfe Valley Times, on 2 November 1996.*

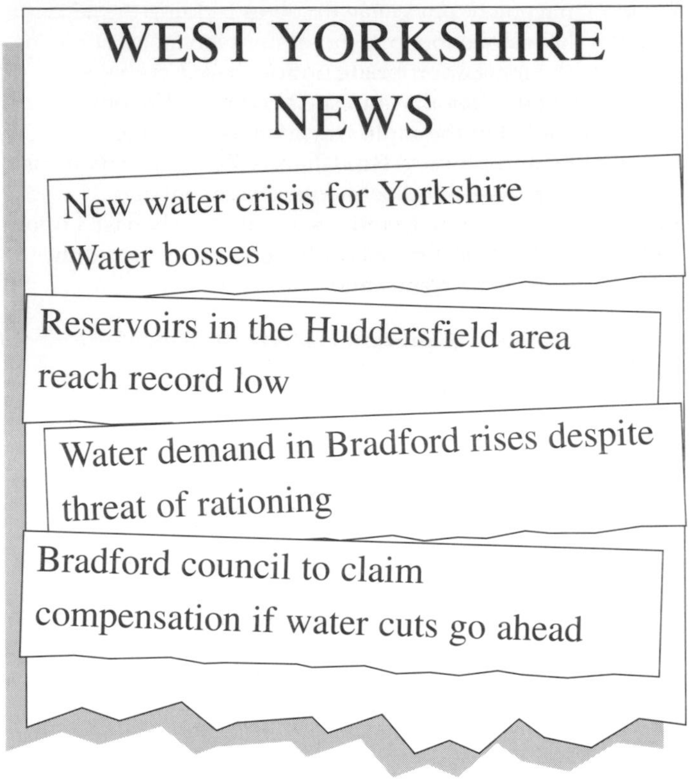

WEST YORKSHIRE NEWS

New water crisis for Yorkshire Water bosses

Reservoirs in the Huddersfield area reach record low

Water demand in Bradford rises despite threat of rationing

Bradford council to claim compensation if water cuts go ahead

Fig 3.12   *Newspapers respond to the drought*

TASK BOX

Drought in West Yorkshire - consequences and causes

Read the text on these pages and in section 2.3.
1. Describe briefly the effects of the drought of 1995 in Yorkshire

2. Water shortages can have both natural and human causes: evaluate the case for both. Was it a natural hazard?

3. In what ways is the data used in the advertisement both convincing and carefully chosen?

- We have had a rainfall shortage of 315 mm in the area this summer.
- 1 out of 6 major reservoirs supplying the Bradford area is now empty.
- Remaining reservoirs in West Yorkshire we only 11% to 18% full.

We may need to consider rota cuts in some area and we urgently need you to continue saving water.

3.5 Water supplies in Yorkshire - management

The summer of 1995 really was the driest on record and existing water supply systems could not cope with this. Water leakage was widespread, especially in hilly areas. Yorkshire Water and other companies were much criticised for their handling of this crisis.

The company faced a number of difficulties in responding fully to the situation - these were physical, social, political and environmental, not just economic. Strategies to deal with these difficulties may be short or long term, preventative or curative in nature.

Water firms to blame

Water watchdogs today said the blame for the growing supply crisis lays squarely on the shoulders of the privatised water companies. If the firms had managed demand better and earlier, they would not need to be taking emergency measures.

Fig 3.14   *Were the water companies to blame?*

£70 m to keep Yorkshire's taps running

Yorkshire Water is to spend a further £70 m on measures intended to ensure no taps run dry in the county this summer - regardless of rainfall.

Included in the package, is £40 m to set up a long-called-for emergency link to the huge Kielder Reservoir in Northumberland. However, the company has immediately come under fire from environmental groups.

Currently being built are a series of new links between Yorkshire rivers, e.g. Derwent to Ouse. New pipelines and pumping stations are planned for parts of Calderdale (with a £600,000 pilot, then £30 m long term).

Fig 3.15   *Some of Yorkshire's proposed plans*

Management options available during and after the drought conditions

- construct new reservoirs;
- install meters;
- cut profits, dividends or high salaries;
- repair leaks;
- abstract more water from rivers;
- import water from other areas;
- build pipelines and pumping stations
- restrict or ban non-essential usage;
- make more use of acquifiers;
- increase existing storage capacity.

Fig 3.16   *The options available to Yorkshire water to avoid future water shortages*

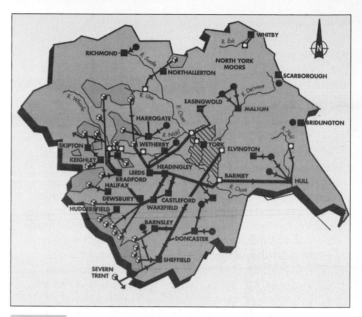

Fig 3.17   *The water grid of Yorkshire*

TECHNIQUES PANEL

A cost-benefit analysis:

This is a standard technique used in most civil engineering decision-making situations to assess whether a scheme is cost effective. It considers **capital and maintenance** costs against three main types of benefit.

Tangible direct benefits can be measured in financial terms and may include savings from reducing or preventing damage to property or to public utilities. **Tangible indirect benefits** relate to financial savings resulting from preserving employment and commercial activity and the provision of emergency services. **Intangible benefits** are not measurable purely financially and may include loss of life, injury, alleviation of fear, ill-health and loss of quality of life, etc.

TASK BOX

Managing drought

1. Evaluate water management in Yorkshire, using headings such as physical, environmental, social, political and economic:
(a) before the summer of 1995
(b) during the drought
(c) since then and in future plans

2. Complete a cost-benefit analysis of the plans (see panel)

3. The grid in Figure 3.17 is central to all of Yorkshire Water's strategies. Describe its general pattern.

3.6 Pollution in rivers

Rivers like the Aire and Calder that enabled the textile industry of the West Riding of Yorkshire to develop, have paid the heavy price of pollution. They have also passed on this legacy into the Humber estuary. The Environment Agency (formerly the NRA) is now charged with the task of putting things right.

Rivers factfile	AIRE	CALDER
Catchment-Area	709 km²	946 km²
River length	148 km	87 km
Population	1,110,000	790,000
Water quality-Good	54%	51%
Fair	15%	23%
Poor	27%	22%
Bad	4%	4%

Figure 3.18: The Rivers Aire and Calder

The river Aire rises beneath Malham Cove in the Karst country of the Yorkshire Dales. It then flows eastwards across the washlands of the upper Aire valley to Keighley. At Saltaire this former source of power is now a 'green lung' between the textile towns. Industrial development in Leeds has done great damage to the river. From here it goes on to join the tidal river Ouse near Goole.

The river Calder has its source in the acidic gritstone moors west of Todmorden, where the steep-sided valleys and the growth of the towns of West Yorkshire have increased the risk of flooding in Calderdale.

The Calder and Aire meet at Castleford, and downstream from here large power stations use river water directly. It has been calculated that their combined discharge carries the sewage of almost 2 million people, and 80 percent of Yorkshire's industrial effluent. Water quality in the upper reaches of both rivers is excellent, and it is used for drinking water. Trout are found here. The biggest sources of pollution today are sewage treatment works.

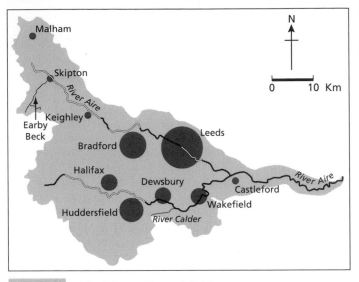

Fig 3.20   *The Rivers Aire and Calder*

Sampling points going downstream	Land use upstream	pH	Temp (C)	Nit-rate mg/l	Phos-phate mg/l	O₂ M Blue	Foam test
1. Sough Bridge	Farmland	8	17	10	25	9	5
2. Rostle Top Road	Housing	8	17	10	25	4	15
3. Wardle Storeys	Factory	7.8	17	20	25	6	50
4. Earby W T W	Sewage wks	7.8	17	100	50	2	45
5. Booth Bridge Farm	Farming	8.6	22	50	50	3	30
6. Brown House Farm	Farming	8.3	17	50	50	4	30
7. Thornton	Housing	8.4	17	50	25	7	15
8. Elslack Bridge	Farming	9	15	20	10	8	10

Foam tests indicate the general level of pollution and the figures are the time in minutes it takes for a shaken sample to lose its foam: longer time = more pollution.

Oxygen content is measured by adding Methylene blue to water sampled and the figures are the number of days which it took for the dye to clear: longer time = less pollution.

Fig 3.19   *Pollution figures for the Rivers Aire and Calder*

TASK BOX

The Aire and Calder

1. Compare the rivers and their pollution problems.

2. Summarise the results of the student's small scale investigation into pollution in Earby Beck. What are the limitations of this and how would you improve it?

The Humber Estuary

Freshwater input is from the Rivers Ouse and Trent. The relative importance of these is shown below in Figure 3.22. In North Yorkshire, a large amount of water is abstracted from the Ouse to supply industries and homes further south, and the river and its tributaries may have their dry weather discharges reduced below the Q as figure. Conversely in West Yorkshire, the rivers Aire, Calder and Don can have their dry weather flows increased by the return of treated effluent. The Trent also receives water artificially from the Severn. This may soon happen to the Ouse when Yorkshire Water begin to receive water from lake Kielder via their proposed Tees-Swale link.

The only other minor inputs are from the river Hull on the north bank of the estuary, and river Ancholme on the south.

Water quality in the estuary is dependent upon this input of freshwater which controls the degree of dilution. Dissolved oxygen level is the key chemical indicator of quality. Effluent from sewage treatment works on the Aire and Don, industrial discharges in the Selby area, and runoff from various agricultural areas, all end up in the estuary. As the largest freshwater input into the North Sea from the English coast, it carries a significant load of heavy metals and nutrients (see data below).

However, it does have a relatively clean bill of health, as the major fish breeding and nursery areas offshore show. The reason for concern is the large scale of development planned along the estuary (see Chapter 7), and the apparent decline in water quality of the southern section of the North Sea.

TASK BOX

The Humber estuary

1. Outline the nature of the chemical pollution within the estuary and beyond

2. Draw a sketch map of the estuary's hinterland and annotate it to show the pattern and possible sources of this pollution

3. Suggest what other evidence about pollution the Environment Agency (and the A-level student) might decide to monitor or collect

4. Research what strategies the Environment Agency adopts to deal with water quality and pollution

---

TASK BOX

Review essays

Choose one of these essays to discuss and plan
Resources - 'Water, too much or too little.' New approaches to managing water must consider not only the issue of preventing flooding, but how to preserve and manage supplies for water shortages.
Hazards - Compare: winter weather, river floods, and drought - in what ways do they need differing responses?
Pollution - Is water pollution a largely unavoidable and inevitable product of economic development?

Fig 3.21 *What influences the level of pollution?*

Pollution levels and types on the Humber Estuary **Fig 3.22**

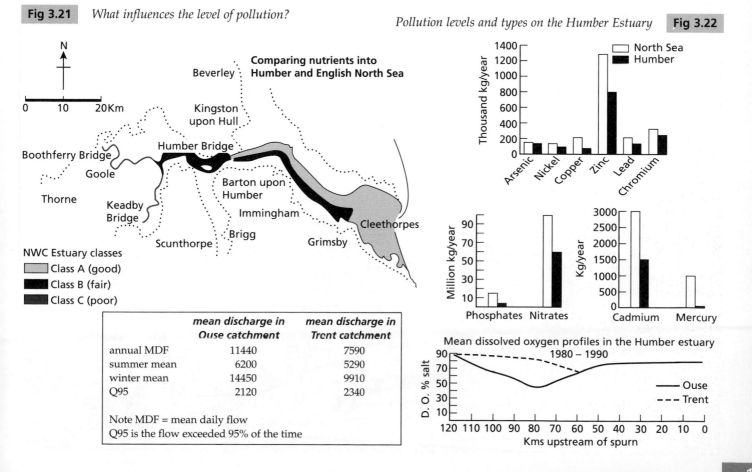

	mean discharge in Ouse catchment	mean discharge in Trent catchment
annual MDF	11440	7590
summer mean	6200	5290
winter mean	14450	9910
Q95	2120	2340

Note MDF = mean daily flow
Q95 is the flow exceeded 95% of the time

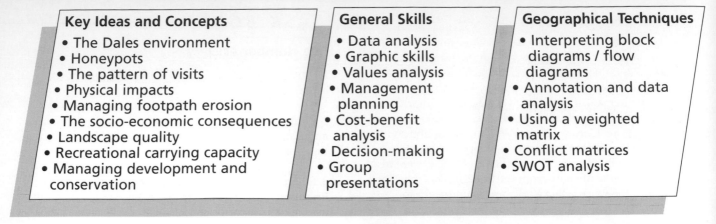

Key Ideas and Concepts
- The Dales environment
- Honeypots
- The pattern of visits
- Physical impacts
- Managing footpath erosion
- The socio-economic consequences
- Landscape quality
- Recreational carrying capacity
- Managing development and conservation

General Skills
- Data analysis
- Graphic skills
- Values analysis
- Management planning
- Cost-benefit analysis
- Decision-making
- Group presentations

Geographical Techniques
- Interpreting block diagrams / flow diagrams
- Annotation and data analysis
- Using a weighted matrix
- Conflict matrices
- SWOT analysis

4.1 The Dales environment

'The Yorkshire Dales is a unique and beautiful place and it is the duty of the Yorkshire Dales National Park Committee to preserve and enhance that living and working landscape whilst encouraging the public to enjoy the area for quiet recreation.'
Robert Heseltine, Chairman Yorkshire Dales National Park 1993

This would seem to be an almost impossible task: to protect the natural beauty and unspoilt quality of 'honeypots' like Malham yet provide facilities for the growing number of summer visitors, whilst not forgetting the needs of those living and working in the Park. This chapter looks closely at the various dilemmas faced by decision makers trying to manage development both within, and adjacent to, the western edge of one of Yorkshire's three National Parks. The underlying issue is that The Dales needs the tourism to support its traditional industries, but can it cope with the physical, social and economic impacts this development brings?

The Three Peaks (mostly SSSI)

The Three Peaks area of the Yorkshire Dales covers about 160 square kilometres of upland. Whernside, Ingleborough and Penyghent owe their distinctive scenery to a combination of physical and human factors. The impacts of grazing, quarrying and settlement are as important as the limestone geology, sub-alpine climate and the legacy of glaciation, when trying to explain this unique mosaic of landscapes. The value of this landscape is such that over 60% of the Three Peaks area is now designated as Sites of special Scientific Interest.

TASK BOX

The Dales environment

Use the resources on this page and those on the inside back cover of this book. Work as a group to –
1. Identify each of the landscapes shown. Explain the nature of each, why it is at risk and why it is worth protecting.

One example has been done for you on the inside back cover.

Fig 4.1 *The variety of landscapes in Yorkshire Dales National Park*

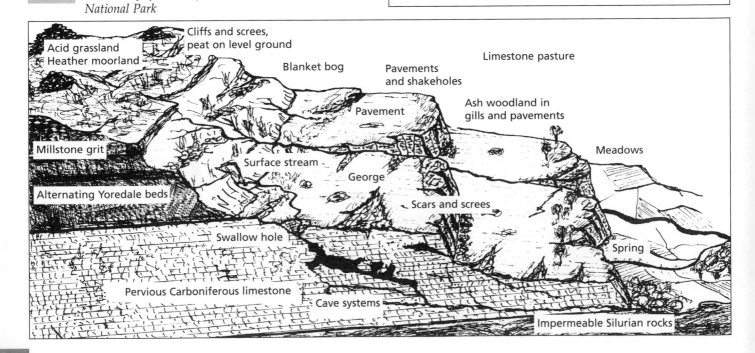

4.2 The pattern of visits

The hot summer of 1995 probably lifted the annual number of visitors to the Yorkshire Dales to almost 10 million. In the Three Peaks area, 80 000 walkers tackled Penyghent, and 32 000 the Three Peaks Challenge.

TASK BOX

The pattern of visits

A variety of primary and secondary data has been collected on this part of the Yorkshire Dales National Park . Using the data:
1. Graph and map results from the spreadsheet.
2. Analyse the pattern of visits using all the data and graphs.
3. Suggest questions you would want to ask about the data and graphs before you make decisions based upon them.

Fig 4.2 *A selection of statistics about visitors to the Yorkshire Dales*

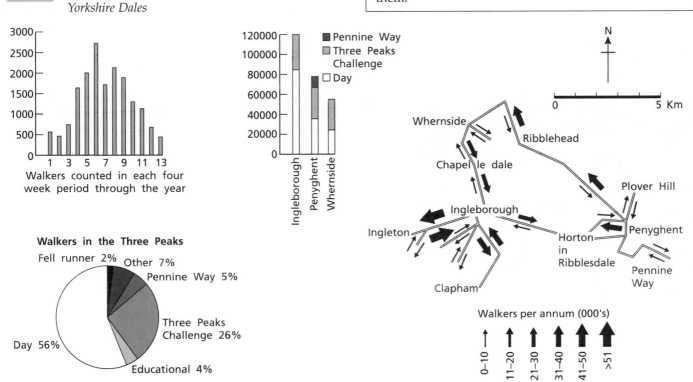

Home origin of the Dale's 8 million yearly UK visitors		Activities enjoyed by these same visitors		Reason for travelling given by Settle-Carlisle rail passengers		Type of Accommodation used by Dales' visitors	
UK Regions	**%**	**Main Activity**	**%**	**Reason**	**Number**	**Type**	**%**
York and Humberside	39	Touring	64	Pleasure trip on the line	1352	Self-catering	26
North West	17	Walking	20	Holiday	182	Caravan (tourer)	17
North	10	Visiting friends	5.3	Going shopping	104	Guesthouse	13
South East	8.2	Passive pursuits	2.3	Not answered	85	Camping	10
East Midlands	4.9	Other	2.1	Visiting friends/relatives	83	Hotel	8.5
East Anglia	4.5	Work	1.3	Sport or entertainment	55	Caravan (static)	7.3
West Midlands	3.9	Active pursuits	1.3	Personal reasons	24	With friends	6.5
Overseas	3.9	Eating out	1.0	Travelling to work	9	Inn	3.1
Greater London	3.2	Educational	0.9	On business	8	Farmhouse	3.1
South West	3.0	Climbing or caving	0.7	Other	7	Youth hostel	2.8
Scotland	2.1	Fishing	0.5	School of college	3	Second home	1.3
Wales	0.9					Other	0.6
Northern Ireland	0.2			TOTAL	1973	Dales Barn	0.5

Home origin of the Dale's 5.2 million yearly Northern visitors		Time spent by visitors in the Dales				Bank holiday parking totals at 5 sites in the western Dales	
Northern Regions	**%**	**Day visitors**	**%**	**Staying visitors**	**%**	**Car parking sites**	**No.**
West Yorkshire	21.7	Over 4 hours	58.9	5–7 days	41.2	Malham (park and grass)	220
Lancashire	10.0	3–4 hours	19.3	2–4 days	33.7	Stainforth (park)	26
North Yorkshire	9.8	1–2 hours	17.0	Over 7 days	20.2	Horton (park and roadside)	86
South Yorkshire	7.0	Less than 1 hour	4.8	1 day	4.9	Ribblehead (roadside)	62
Cumbria	2.2					Kilnsey (roadside)	6

4.3 Physical impacts on the environment

The Three Peaks area of the Yorkshire Dales has become a magnet for walkers of all types: ranging from family strolls in the wooded valleys, to more determined forays up onto the limestone plateau and windswept hilltops, where hardy long distance walkers can attempt the 'Three Peaks Challenge'.

The high rainfall, poor drainage, and thousands of boots trampling the fragile vegetation are a devastating combination. On the peaty upper slopes, waterlogged ground, deep gullies and numerous soil slides, have led to severe localised erosion. Whernside is perhaps the least damaged of the three peaks.

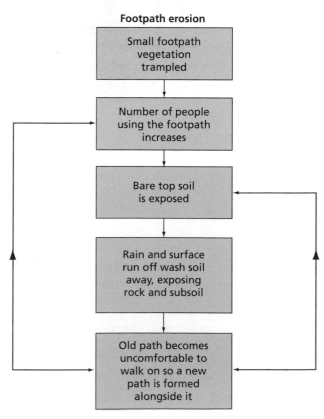

Fig 4.3 *Laying wooden walkways helps to prevent footpath erosion*

Footpath erosion

- Small footpath vegetation trampled
- Number of people using the footpath increases
- Bare top soil is exposed
- Rain and surface run off wash soil away, exposing rock and subsoil
- Old path becomes uncomfortable to walk on so a new path is formed alongside it

Fig 4.5 *The cycle of footpath erosion*

Three Peaks rescue bid is underway

'The worst footpath erosion I have every seen anywhere in this country' is how Dr Neil Bayfield of the Institute of Terrestrial Ecology summed up his report to the Yorkshire Dales N. P. Committee on the devastation caused by walkers in the Three Peaks area of the Park.

He discovered that most paths across this wild upland have been trampled into a boggy morass, with an average width of 11.4 metres – twice the width of a 'B' class road. In one place, a path has been eroded to 150 metres wide. Now armed with these shocking facts, the National Park Committee has embarked on a massive rescue operation in unprecedented scale and complexity, costing hundreds of thousands of pounds.

Reconnaissance undertaken that year confirmed the worst fears. Of the 63 km of footpaths that gave access to the Peaks, more than 24 km were in a severely damaged state. A further 30 km required remedial work if progressive erosion on a similar scale was to be avoided.

Craven Herald, June 1986

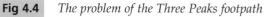

Fig 4.4 *The problem of the Three Peaks footpath*

TASK BOX

The physical impacts

Use the maps from Chapter 1, those inside the front cover, the flow diagram from Figure 4.2, and the resources on this page to answer these questions.

1. Describe the nature of the Three Peaks footpath erosion problem. Explain the physical and human factors involved.

2. A carrying capacity of 50 000 walkers p.a. may well be critical in triggering severe erosion: explain this and relate it to Figures 4.2 – 4.6.

F	F	H	F	F	P	B	B	A	B	B	A	B	B	B	A	B	A	A	B	A	A	A	A	A	H	M	M
F	F	F	F	F	P	P	P	B	A	B	B	B	P	A	B	B	B	B	A	P	A	A	A	A	H	M	M
H	H	F	F	P	P	P	B	A	A	B	B	A	A	A	B	B	A	A	A	A	A	A	H	P	P	F	
F	F	F	F	F	P	B	B	A	A	A	B	B	A	A	B	B	A	A	A	A	A	A	H	H	F	F	
F	H	M	M	M	P	A	A	B	B	A	A	B	B	A	B	A	B	B	B	A	A	A	A	A	H	H	C	P
H	M	M	M	M	P	B	A	B	B	A	B	A	A	A	A	B	A	A	P	A	A	A	H	S	S	S	P
F	M	M	M	M	P	A	AA	B	A	A	B	B	B	A	B	A	A	A	A	A	A	A	A	A	S	S	B	P
M	M	M	H	M	P	A	B	B	B	B	A	B	B	A	B	A	A	B	A	P	A	A	A	H	S	S	S	M
M	M	M	H	F	P	B	B	B	B	B	B	B	B	A	B	B	B	A	A	A	P	P	A	A	A	H	H	H	H	M
M	M	M	H	M	P	P	B	A	B	A	B	B	B	A	B	A	A	A	A	A	A	A	A	H	H	H	S	M

F=Sheeps Fescue	H=Health Rush	C=Common Sedge	B=Bare soil
M=Matt Grass	P= Planted Rye Grass	S=Soft Rush	A=Aggregate

Fig 4.6 *A quadrat 30 × 10 showing how a once entirely bare soil footpath is recovering.*

4.4 Managing footpath erosion

The Three Peaks Project, begun in 1987 as a research project, has led to a variety of initiatives that have helped combat footpath erosion and habitat damage. It has been undertaken by the Yorkshire Dales National Park in partnership with the Countryside Commission, English Nature and the Sports Council, with much assistance from the local community, user groups, volunteers, and the commercial sector. The RAF has also provided helicopter support for the more remote or sensitive sites.

As well as providing and maintaining the footpath network for the recreational user, there were other criteria to be met. These included minimal environmental impact, cost-effectiveness in construction and minimal maintenance.

Fig 4.8

Other methods

Sticking to principles

Repair of the Three Peaks paths began properly in April 1987. The awesome task fell to a team led by Simon Rose. The future of the Three Peaks was very much in their hands.

However, at the start of the project it was not clear exactly how the stricken paths should be repaired. Many of them were across wet peat and rebuilding would be a nightmare.

A range of possible techniques was open to the Three Peaks team, including boardwalks, the use of stone aggregate (chippings), laying plastic rafts over the peat, and mixing a hardening chemical into it.

"In rebuilding the paths we have to keep a number of principles in mind," says Simon. Techniques have to be chosen to minimise the impact on the landscape. "Whatever we do it must not look too obtrusive, walkers want it to look as 'natural' as possible, and quite right too."

The ecology of the Three Peaks also has to be safeguarded. The wetness of the area has contributed to the footpath problems and it might be that drainage would be a good idea to improve the state of the paths. However, the flora of this area is distinctive partly because of the wet conditions and any ill-considered drainage would alter the plant community.

The major other consideration is the logistics of the project. Movement of stone and other materials to remote fellsides could cause more damage than was there already. The scale of work is such - the project is the largest yet seen on peat soils - that it has to be as mechanised as possible.

"We are having to start at the bottom of the fells and move up and not necessarily tackle the worst bits first," explains Simon. "The paths we're building have to be wide enough and durable enough to take diggers and dumper trucks."

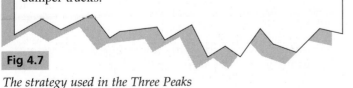

Fig 4.7

The strategy used in the Three Peaks

Fig 4.9   *Why might some people object to this type of repair?*

TASK BOX

Footpath management

1. Make a 10 × 30 grid to display the quadrat data opposite. Shade it as follows:
   - wild grasses (fescue and matt) green
   - planted grass (rye) yellow
   - wetland plants (rushes and sedge) blue
   - bare soil (means erosion) brown
   - aggregate (put down by N. Park staff) black

2. Explain what has been happening and why the N. Park officials are pleased so far.

The Main Restoration Techniques

Description	Conditions most used in	Gradient	Life expectancy	Other information
A. Boardwalk: Wooden boards floated over deep peat or placed on legs.	High moisture content bogs, standing water or peat.	Suited to level areas or slopes less than 10 degrees.	About 20 years.	Difficult transport, high cost, high labour input. 10 metres laid per day (5 skilled workers).
B. Flexboard: Similar to above, hardwood placed onto the ground and fixed in position.	Any soils (as above).	Slight to moderate slopes up to 15 degrees.	15–20 years.	Difficult to transport, low labour input. 200 metres laid per day (4 skilled workers).
C. Geotextiles aggregate path: Engineered path of woven plastic mat covered with crushed stone.	Any soils, can be built on thin or deep peat.	From level ground to 25 degrees.	Indefinite but needs maintenance.	Difficult to transport heavy machinery to the site. Paths must support their weight, high labour input. 100 metres laid per day (5 skilled workers).
D. Stone-pitched path: Stones placed two-thirds below ground level and stepped.	Well-drained. Best on steep slopes with a subsoil base.	All levels to about 40 degrees of slope.	Indefinite. Very little maintenance required.	High cost. High labour input. 10 metres laid per day (5 skilled workers).
E. Subsoil path: Involves mechanised excavation of subsoil and burial of turf (Inversion).	Shallow peat with suitable subsoil which should have a good stone and clay content.	All levels to about 30 degrees of slope.	Indefinite with some maintenance.	Low cost, low labour input. 100 metres laid per day (1 skilled Hymac digger and operator). £3.50 per metre.

Fig 4.10   *Comparison of different techniques*

TECHNIQUES PANEL

A weighted matrix

You will need a copy of the matrix below.

1. Decide on a rank order of criteria (the rows) below, and weight them from 5 downwards, e.g. if you think lower costs are most important, then that will be 5.

2. Consider each of the five techniques (columns) in turn under each of the weighted headings, and score them out of 10, e.g. subsoil path-is cheapest so score 10.

3. Multiply the scores in each cell by their weightings, e.g. 5 × 10 = 50 and add up the totals of each column.

4. Highest total means 'best' technique

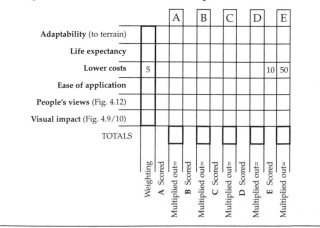

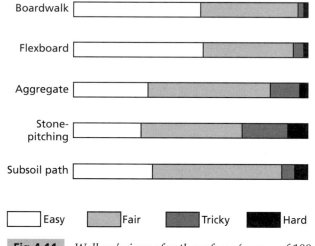

Fig 4.11   *Walkers' views of path surfaces (survey of 100 walkers on Penyghent*

Notes on a visit to Penyghent with N. P. Field officer
Three Peaks pedestrian count at 250,000 count at 250,000. Estimated 3 to 4% increase per annum. 1992 survey estimated 6 million visitors to the area. Spending approx. £8 each – £48 million for benefit of 18,000 residents?

TASK BOX

Footpath management

1. Outline the nature of restoration techniques used in the Three Peaks area.

2. Construct a weighed matrix (technique panel) and use it to evaluate the various repair techniques.

4.5 Social and economic consequences

The Yorkshire Dales are a magnet for visitors from all over Britain, but so the local people suffer or benefit from this? Whilst on one hand there are obvious economic benefits in employment and business, there are often social and environmental costs for other residents in the same village.

Park remains firm on second home policy

National Park planners are defying governmental advice in their drive to stop the growth of holiday homes in the Dales. The committee is determined to stick to its policy that new homes in the area should be the principal residency of the occupier - not second homes.

Councillor Shelagh Marshall told members at the meeting on Tuesday that in some villages half of all homes were second properties.

Chairman Robert Heseltine said: "We are trying to obtain affordable housing for local people."

Vice-chairman Ralph Atkinson expressed concern about the effect on rural services of the growth in second homes, particularly schools, health services and village shops.

Craven Herald, 12 May 95

New link to cut cars

The Daleslink bus service hits the road tomorrow, running between Settle, Ingleton and Malham in a bid to reduce the number of cars on local routes.

Craven Herald, 26 May 1995

Fig 4.12 *The problem of day-trippers, drivers and second-homers*

Tourist honeypot loses its attraction

Tourists are vital to the economic future of the Yorkshire Dales – not the kind who currently make up the large majority of visitors to the region.

The Dales are still attracting too many day-trippers and not enough who spend several days in the region, according to speakers at a conference on the effects of tourism held in Settle this week. Day-trippers, though welcome, spend an average of £13 per visit. It was vital to encourage tourists to use the Dales as a short break location. 'Those kind of tourists provide a far bigger boost to the local economy. As well as using hotels and guest houses, they spend far more money and spread it more widely.'

Yorkshire Post, 25 September 1995

Fig 4.13 *100 Tourists' views of services and 50 residents' views of tourists*

TASK BOX

Social and economic effects

1. Copy and complete the Conflict Matrix, adding at least two other likely 'roles' (see techniques panel overleaf).

2. Set out the positive and negative social and economic consequences of increased tourist activity in Clapham. Does Clapham gain or lose?

Fig 4.14 *Tourist signs near Clapham village*

A very English muddle is tearing apart a village in the Yorkshire Dales

The village is Clapham. It's a time-stopped spot, where winter has barely turned to spring. The loudest sound is the bubbling, cascading beck which runs the length of the main street. Hardly anything stirs early in the May mulchy mornings. The first squelch of the first fell-walker's boots aren't heard till after breakfast. Cafes come out of hibernation and struggle to open for morning coffee at about 11.

Landlord of the New Inn, Keith Mannion, is one of the local business community who contributed to the £4,000 cost of three new signs which he hopes will contribute to Clapham's prosperity. New signs are vital, Mannion says, because the village needs tourism as well as commuters...

The question is how much tourism should Clapham allow? Is there anything it can do to regulate the flow of visitors and the influence they have on the place, and what do they contribute to the local economy?

'It's a mixed blessing being on the edge of the Dales,' says one resident. With agriculture in decline, tourism is necessary, but the new signs will encourage coachloads and carloads of people who will not necessarily spend very much, and possibly not stay overnight in Clapham.

Guardian 'omnibus', 2 May 1996

TECHNIQUES PANEL

A conflict matrix

In its simplest form, crosses are placed in a conflict matrix to identify where people or land uses may conflict with each other, for example, residents and the owners of tourist shops. In more complex forms, scores could be written in to reflect the severity of the conflict: e.g. +1 or +2 = agreement: 0 = neutral: -1 or -2 = conflict. Seasonal impacts will score less.

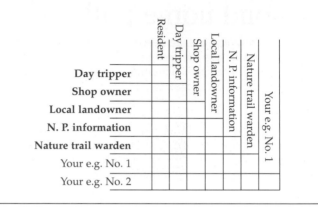

	Resident	Day tripper	Shop owner	Local landowner	N. P. information	Nature trail warden	Your e.g. No. 1
Day tripper							
Shop owner							
Local landowner							
N. P. information							
Nature trail warden							
Your e.g. No. 1							
Your e.g. No. 2							

Fig 4.15   *Village divided over tourist development*

The importance of tourism   **Fig 4.16**

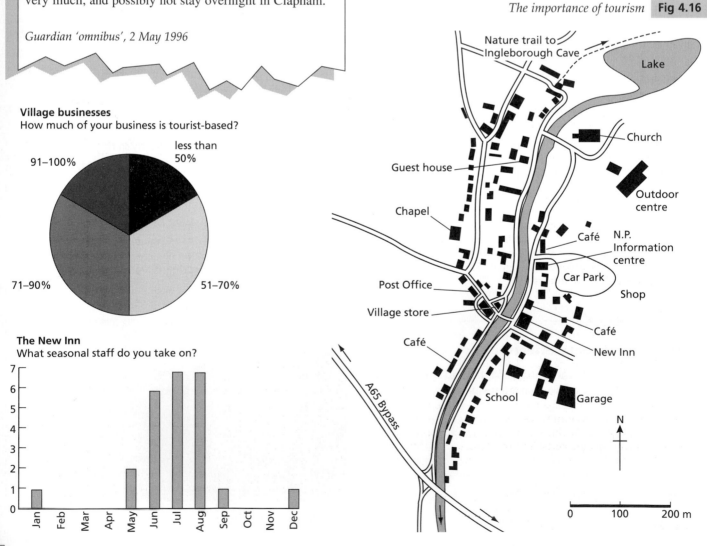

Village businesses
How much of your business is tourist-based?

- less than 50%
- 51–70%
- 71–90%
- 91–100%

The New Inn
What seasonal staff do you take on?

4.6 Managing development and conservation

This is a decision-making exercise based on proposals to develop the southern end of the Settle-Carlisle Railway.

There is a range of options proposed at each of three sites along the railway. Whilst there are those locally who would welcome a bigger tourist development in Ribblesdale, there are others who wish to conserve the traditions and unspoilt nature of this 'gateway' to the Dales.

The area is rich both in scenery and in industrial archaeology. Tourism in the area is growing and traffic problems are beginning to become significant. Vehicles in the Park could double in the next 25 years.

The Railway would seem to offer an alternative means of access for visitors.

Fig 4.17   *The spectacular Ribblehead viaduct on the Settle-Carlisle line*

TASK BOX

Managing tourist development and conservation

Using Ordnance Survey maps the newspaper article below, and the resources on the pages that follow:
1. Make a bullet point list of the main issues involved.
2. Identify and explain the differing views of people
3. Analyse the options at each of the three sites, either:
　　(i) using a **cost-benefit analysis** (section 3.5), or
　　(ii) an **environmental impact analysis** (see section 7.6), or
　　(iii) a **'SWOT' analysis** (see techniques panel over).
4. Outline and justify your choice of developments

Park's key role in preserving our heritage

The Settle-Carlisle line is one of the best known railway routes in the country.

It was built by the Midland Railway Company as a main line route to Scotland. Completed in 1875, it had taken six years and £3.5 million to build.

At the peak of construction, 7000 'navvies' were employed, housed in camps or 'settlements', the main cluster of these was around Ribblehead viaduct at Batty Moss.

The navvies had to endure hardship and dangers: the line, 72 miles in length, with 20 major viaducts and 14 tunnels, is a fitting memorial to their endeavour.

The spectacular engineering is only one of the features that makes the Settle-Carlisle line special. Its route through some of England's most dramatic and picturesque scenery is another, but third is the extent to which the distinctive Midland Railway Company's buildings, have survived intact.

In 1991, the whole route was designated an 'area of special architectural or historic interest'.

The scheme is jointly funded by the National Park Authority, Craven and Eden District Councils, Carlisle City Council and English Heritage.

The scheme is helping to fund a range of important projects in the National Park. Other funding is being sought from the Railway Heritage Trust. Friends of the Settle-Carlisle Railway Trust, the European Union, the Heritage Lottery Fund as well as Railtrack and Regional Railways.

The stone-built waiting shelters at Horton-in-Ribblesdale and Dent stations have been fully restored, including reinstatement of their architectural details, such as ridge tiles and ornamental bargeboards. Improved platform lighting is being planned for these stations and six others along the line.

Proposals are well advanced to restore the station at Ribblehead and to improve the appearance of the station area. Besides providing facilities for passengers, the station will have information and displays explaining the history of the line and interpreting the Ribblehead area.

The National Park Authority is also taking the lead in developing a major project at Langcliffe Quarry, which is adjacent to the Settle–Carlisle line just north of Settle.

The site contains the massive Hoffmann Lime Kiln, the largest and one of the best preserved examples in the country, as well as other industrial and archaeological features. The site has significant nature conservation importance too.

Other developments are happening elsewhere along the line around Hellifield station. The beautifully restored Victorian station has recently been brought into fuller use and there are plans to develop major leisure facilities on adjoining land.

Whilst strictly just beyond the Settle–Carlisle line, Hellifield will nevertheless become an important 'gateway' to the line and to the Yorkshire Dales National Park.

At a time when ever more cars are using Dales roads, the National Park Authority sees the Settle–Carlisle line as offering an alternative, convenient and less damaging means of access to the National Park for visitors.

County Times, Craven Herald, September 1996

Fig 4.18   *Plans for upper Ribblesdale*

Hellifield Station site

Mr J Winder (a farmer, whose land is being used to help develop the site)
"The village needs new life breathing into it."

Mr D Pinner (local Planning Officer)
"This village needs investment to reverse the decline of the last 30 years. The Centre's new jobs will replace the railway-based ones of the past, and new housing on the old auction mart will allow population growth."

Mrs F Sample (resident)
"The new bypass and access road will make it quieter through the village, but more importantly the railway development will bring new jobs."

Option 1 - Station Railway Centre

Development will be concentrated here, outside the National Park, at the entrance to the Settle-Carlisle corridor. It involves the development of the area within and immediately next to the station. The scheme will create 38 full time jobs, 10 new businesses, 4500 m³ floorspace, and 5 ha of development land. European Upland area funding (5b) will be attracted together with any commercial sector investment. Projected incomes from these activities and growth in the Ribblesdale visitor market could reach £485 000 p.a. following completion.
Capital costs:
Construction of Heritage Centre £150 000
Construction - engine shed workshop £1.25 million
Car parking and service road £125 000
Relocating of engineering depot £275 000
Construction of new access road £255 000
Sliproad - proposed Hellifield bypass £150 000

Option 2 - Railway Centre and Rural Recreation Centre

This will consist of the above scheme together with the greater involvement of commercial sector development to provide a hotel, holiday village and showground. There is the potential to create a further 60 jobs and to generate £1 200 000 from day visitors and £1 140 000 from staying visitors.
Capital costs:
Option I costs
Plus a further £2 000 000 from the private sector.

TASK BOX

Review essay

Answer one of these essays:
(a) 'the environmental costs of increased recreation and tourism at honeypot sites outweigh the economic and social benefits they bring.'
(b) 'developments in recreation and tourism can lead to conflicts of interest. What strategies are there to manage these conflicts?'

Mr P Brown (YDNP, Planning Officer)
"The Authority recognises the focal importance of Hellifield station. The refurbished, listed station will provide an attractive and fitting gateway to the line and the wider area of the corridor. Development of the land adjacent to the station could reinforce its position and role."

Nr E J Stott (Chairman, Settle and Carlisle Railway Development Company)
"I am delighted to offer you our full support. A critical ingredient to the successful development of the Hellifield project will be strong public and private sector partnership".

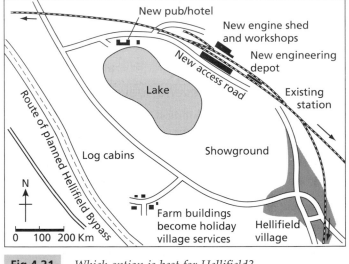

Fig 4.21   *Which option is best for Hellifield?*

TECHNIQUES PANEL

Essay skills

Writing a good essay involves a number of activities and elements that are reflected in the markscheme:
- an initial brainstorm and rough plan of the essay
- a clear introduction to define question and terms
- the argument of the essay must be supported by a range of relevant case studies that provide evidence for points made.
- analyse means 'critically investigate' not list facts
- evaluate in a conclusion means make a judgement based on the evidence and ideas you have used.
- make use of the atlas, sketch maps and diagrams

<table>
<tr><td>

Key Ideas and Concepts
- Changing industrial structure
- Changing locations
- Inner city industrial redevelopment
- Greenfield development
- Redevelopment and conservation
- Patterns of industry in the city

</td><td>

General Skills
- Data analysis
- Mapping skills
- Data representation
- Fieldwork activities
- Decision-making
- Group presentations

</td><td>

Geographical Techniques
- Location quotients
- Map analysis
- Aerial photo analysis
- Fieldwork suggestions
- Sketch maps
- Annotating sketches

</td></tr>
</table>

5.1 Changing structure

Yorkshire's farming has traditionally been associated with the primary production of wool, and the Bradford region with the manufacture of woollen textiles.

However, as demand for these products has fallen, global markets have shifted, and new technology has arrived, the city has had to adapt to these challenges and develop its service and quaternary sectors.

The traditional factors of industrial locations, such as water supply and power, transport of raw materials by canal, and the need for a large local labour force, have given way to the new emphases on fast road access, cheap land and the opportunity to expand.

Industrial location

A number of theories have been put forward to explain the location of industry. One of the most famous was that of Alfred Weber. This showed how the location of many larger secondary industries were tied to the raw materials they used, and how the weight of these greatly influenced transport costs. Firms were assumed to always choose the 'least-cost location'.

However, for the lighter manufacturing and tertiary industries of today, the decision-making process is often much more complex. Footloose, market-oriented companies may be attracted to inner city areas where urban development has created prime sites offering grants from government or local authorities. Alternatively, they may relocate to the rural-urban fringes of cities where greenfield sites offer easy expansion.

TECHNIQUES PANEL

Calculating industrial location quotients:

Industrial location quotients offer a measure of the degree of specialisation which an area shows. To calculate the quotient use the following formula:

$$ILO = \dfrac{\dfrac{\text{Number of people employed in textiles in Bradford}}{\text{Number of people employed in textiles in the UK}}}{\dfrac{\text{Number of people employed in industries in Bradford}}{\text{Number of people employed in all industries in UK}}}$$

A value of 1 will represent the national average. A large number indicates a marked degree of specialisation, whereas a value of less than 1 means employment is likely to be much more diversified.

TASK BOX

Changing structure

1. Draw divided bar graphs to compare the changing pattern of the FOUR employment sectors in Bradford in 1851, 1901, 1951 and 1991.

2. Describe the trends shown and relate them to the changes in textiles over the same period and suggest the likely causes and the consequences of these changes.

3. Calculate the *location quotients* for each year and briefly comment on them.

Number of people employed in Bradford's	1851	1901	1951	1991
PRIMARY	2654	5577	911	280
SECONDARY	41745	77199	88619	24080
TERTIARY	15058	62114	70322	155760
QUATERNARY	0	0	0	900
TOTAL	59457	144890	159852	181020
BRADFORD TEXTILES	33484	46403	39379	4480
UK TEXTILES	295276	122069	188773	26140
BRADFORD INDUSTRIES	59457	144890	159852	181020
UK INDUSTRIES	10207236	14328727	22213652	23452230

Fig 5.1

The changing pattern of industry and employment in Bradford

5.2 Changing locations

The locations of the past are different form those of today, as this contrast of a traditional site at Saltaire and a modern footloose site at Euroway clearly show.

Saltaire - a traditional location

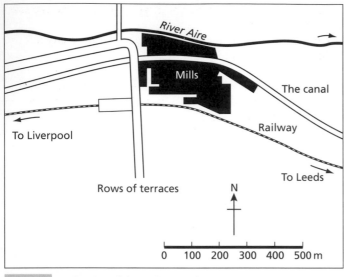

Fig 5.2   *The site of the mills at Saltaire*

1n 1853, Sir Titus Salt built a large woollen mill on the then greenfield site to the north of Bradford. He chose what was the classic site for a textile mill. Around his mill he built a village, which he called Saltaire, to house his 800 workers and their families. Besides the houses he also provided a school, a chapel, a hospital and a library (see section 5.5).

Euroway - a modern footloose location

Fig 5.3   *The motorway exit to Euroway*

In 1988, Bradford City Council encouraged the setting up of a large trading estate to the south of the city, by releasing land for development. It offered incentives and supported applications for Regional Selective Assistant Grants (totalling £1.2 million in 1992), so an area that had previously been farmland was soon taken over by large companies, mostly in the tertiary sector, all recognising the potential of this 'greenfield' location. The estate continues to grow both in area and the number of firms involved.

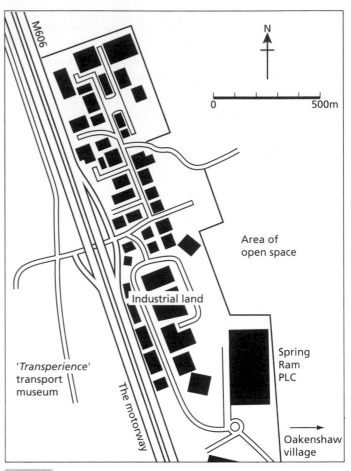

Fig 5.4   *The site of Euroway*

Fig 5.5

The mill on the side of the canal

┌─ **TASK BOX** ─────────────────┐

Changing locations

1. Contrast briefly the two sites shown: the industries involved and the location factors which might have operated there, and why they may no longer be advantageous.

2. In what ways is Saltaire not typical of other nineteenth century industrial communities?

5.3 Inner city redevelopment

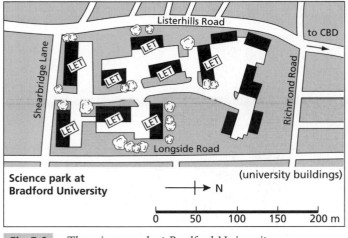

Fig 5.6   *The science park at Bradford University*

TASK BOX

Inner city industrial redevelopment

1. Using resources from this and the next page, and the field work database in section 5.6, set out:
(a) the nature of these two adjacent areas and the types of firms they attract
(b) the advantages and disadvantages of inner city sites like Listerhills and Brownroyd.

2. Draw an annotated sketch of the aerial photograph of Brownroyd. Show land uses, buildings, roads, and the factors that might be important to new or expanding businesses.

Listerhills Science Park

In recent years, Bradford has worked hard to improve the environment of its inner city areas, sweeping away the Victorian legacy of slum terraced housing and derelict textile mills. New roads have been built, and sites cleared and made available to developers.

With grants available from government and local councils, larger companies were attracted to the sites at Brownroyd and smaller ones to the Listerhills Science Park. Set up in 1983 by the partnership of Bradford University, Bradford Metropolitan Council and English Estates, the four-hectare Park site cost £200 000 plus fees and the five phases of building have since cost in the region of £4 million. Rents are currently at £6.34 per sq. ft., with additional fees for maintenance and site security. All this is within a mile of the busy central business district.

Eltec

Eltec computers grew out of the University of Bradford, dealing initially with local education and business customers.

Many similar firms in the quaternary sector were attracted by the 'rent holiday' and the hi-tech premises of the Science Park. Elonex Computers, another nationally known company is also here. In 1990, Eltec moved to the nearby Fieldhead Business Centre looking for lower rents and mixed office/workshop facilities in new premises. They currently employ a staff of 30, and reach an annual turnover of £6 million.

Recently, the company has become part of the Hugh Symons Group PLC, which is a fast growing supplier of computer and communications products from a variety of locations in the UK. Will Eltec move again?

Fig 5.7   *Why did high-tecnology firms set up here?*

Fig 5.8   *Case study of Eltec, a high-technology firm*

Grattan's multi-million pound complex newly installed in its inner city location

Fig 5.9   *The location of Grattan's multi-million pound complex at Listerhills (Brown royd)*

Founded in 1912, the Grattan Mail Order company grew naturally from its roots in the textile trade. Aspect, Scotcade, Kaleidoscope and Next are Grattan partners. However, despite this growth and success, by 1981 the company had some serious problems.

The problems
(1) too many separate and inadequate warehouses
(2) an ordering and record system all on paper
(3) the main Ingleby Road building was on three floors

The options
(1) Move South (to Reading or Swindon perhaps)
(2) Add on to the existing Ingleby Road site
(3) Move locally to a site between Listerhills and Brown royd

The implications
Option (1) expensive, unfair to workforce, and very risky
Option (2) cheap, short term, retained some problems, and would disrupt existing operation
Option (3) was logical, but was a site available? How could it be financed? Would it work?

The site in 1988
- 21 hectare site but owned by various companies
- environmentally poor (mineshafts, quarries, dumps)
- Bradford Beck bisects the site
- flat land is rare in Bradford area
- close to existing offices and warehouses
- inner city area should attract grants
- will preserve jobs locally
- will act as a multiplier for Bradford firms/services
- will mean easier planning permission
- Bradford Council wants the development and jobs
- the total Grattan investment may reach £50 million

The development in 1990
The new complex, opened in 1990, has an area of 80,000 sq. metres including offices, warehousing, generators and transport bays. The interior is fully computerised with automatic conveyors, sorters, scanners and pallet systems. Beyond the mile of service roads there is extensive landscaping.

Fig 5.10   *Some history of Grattan*

5.4 Greenfield development

Euroway Trading Estate

In trying to respond to increasing demands from companies wishing to set up in the Bradford area, the city has permitted a number of peripheral industrial sites to develop and expand. These are closely linked to the growing motorway network.

This has proved to be a popular move commercially, though there is increasing pressure from a variety of environmental groups to limit further development. Trading estates like Euroway which offer very large industrial sites are not compatible with land uses such as agriculture and housing, but recreation in the form of an existing golf course and a new transport museum and park have developed here.

Fig 5.11   *Business park and surrounding greenbelt area*

Spring Ram Corporation PLC

The company has a bathroom, kitchen, furniture and door empire, with a turnover of over £300 million per year, and employs over 5000 people in its factories across Yorkshire and neighbouring regions. In recent years the company has attempted to bring more of its operations together into one single area. With a number of premises on or adjacent to the Euroway Estate, the company has sought to develop southwards onto farmland near to the village of Oakenshaw.

```
TASK BOX
```

Developing greenfield sites

1. Using resources from this page, and the field work database in section 5.6:
(a) briefly describe the nature of the area shown and the types of firms it attracts
(b) draw an annotated sketch of photo 5.11
(c) analyse the advantages and disadvantages of out-of-city sites like Euroway (see Figures 5.3 and 5.4)
(d) identify the possible conflicts (see section 4.5) that new developments like these might create

Go-ahead for greenbelt factories plan

Bathroom giant Spring Ram was today granted permission to build its factories on greenbelt farmland ending a five year battle to keep the company off the land. Bradford Council Planning Committee gave the go-ahead after being told that the authority would face paying millions of pounds in compensation if the application was refused. But the company has lodged a £1.8 million bond with the council as an assurance of extensive landscaping of the complex at Oakenshaw. A countryside park will be created by the time the units open in July 1995.

But Shirley Dewhirst, representing the Residents' Action Group, said after the meeting: "We are appalled. The whole thing has come about because of the promise of jobs three years ago."

Officers today told the committee that the change to three smaller units was technically an amendment that should not be refused.

Bradford South MP Gerry Sutcliffe wrote opposing it and Labour ward councillors Tim Mahon and Tony Cairns pressed for its refusal. They pointed out that job estimates were now only about 130 and described the scheme as speculation.

Councillor Colin Charlesworth (Con) said the company should have been made to submit a fresh application. "We are looking at an entirely different scheme from the one passed previously." Spring Ram financial director Andrew Mackenzie said they would endeavour to be good neighbours to local residents.

Telegraph & Argus, 19 October 1994

Fig 5.12   *Business developments and their impacts*

Previous events

1989 - Company unveils plans for £54 million factory. Local residents protest and plans are withdrawn.

1990 - Revised scheme is submitted. Labour controlled planning committee refused permission, and Bradford's business community condemns action.

1991 - Plans revised again and are this time passed on the casting vote of the chairman. Approval is on condition that there is extensive landscaping. Bradford looks forward to an estimated 1000 jobs.

1993 - Company is financially unable to ahead and local residents celebrate.

1994 - New management at Spring Ram announces plans for three smaller units, with more landscaping, and further from the village.

5.5 Redevelopment and conservation

Fig 5.13

The mill's site and environmental quality

Saltaire scoops national award

The historic village of Saltaire has scooped a top national accolade and has been hailed as a shining beacon of economic regeneration.

The village beat off competition from the Edinburgh Opera House and London's new Waterloo Station for the Civic Trust's prestigious award.

Last night, Salts Mill owner Jonathan Silver and Bradford council conservation officer Steve Bateman picked up the award for planning and regeneration.

The Mill currently houses the Hockney Art Gallery, a furniture store, a restaurant , boutiques and hi-tech company Pace Micro Technology, which employed 900 people. The surrounding area boasts tourist shops and a Grade II listed village of 700 homes.

Bradford Telegraph and Argus, 29 March 1996

TASK BOX

Redevelopment and conservation

Using these resources (and Section 5.2), evaluate the extent to which Saltaire has managed to achieve both redevelopment and conservation.

TASK BOX

Data gathering activities

Look at the locations and ideas suggested below. As a group, discuss how you would plan a similar investigation, in a city or industrial area you know.

Which data will be collected by fieldwork?

(i) name the sites involved and the nature of them, e.g. *Saltaire* north of the city (on A650 near Shipley) a site typical of industry in the past.

Listerhills near the University: a cluster of Hi-tech firms have deliberately chosen inner city developed sites

Brownroyd adjacent but near the inner ring road where large companies have been attracted by space and grants

Euroway South of the city (first exit from the M606) where modern footloose development is attracted by the large greenfield sites, grants and immediate motorway access.

Have alternative ready, e.g. Hillam Rd, Canal Rd, Tong, Bowling.

(ii) decide on the techniques you will use, e.g.
    land use survey

      environmental quality index etc

A still or video camera could be a useful means of both recording and presenting information.

What secondary information you will need?

Name the type of sources involved, e.g.

Ordnance survey maps

City planning department (economic development)

5.6 Patterns of industry

These field work results were collected in September 1995 by questionnaires in three of the four areas already studied.

Name of Company	District	Type of firm	Struc.	Age	Premises	Moved?	From where?	Advantages	Drawbacks	Size	Men	Women
Seabrook Crisps		Crisp Manufacturer	secondary	15	purpose built	No		Central/large site	large	50	150	
Leeming & Peel		Spring Manufacturer	secondary	20	adapted	Yes	Locally	Central		small	7	1
Twinweld Mesh Centre		Wiremesh Manufacturer	secondary	40	adapted	Yes	Locally	Road access / Central	Old premises	small	7	1
Sharps		Floor coverings	secondary	14	adapted	Yes	Locally	Central / Large site		medium	10	2
A E Auto Parts	browrroyd	Car engine parts	secondary	22	adapted	Yes	Locally		Traffic	large	350	0
Lancaster & Winter		Steel stockholders	tertiary	13	adapted	Yes	Locally	Large site / Central	Secondaryurity	medium	10	1
Morrisons PLC		Supermarket & distribution	tertiary	7	purpose built	No		Road access / Market	Traffic	large	30	120
Plumb Centre		Plumbers merchant	tertiary	18	purpose built	Yes	Locally	Large site	Traffic	medium	9	2
Grattans PLC		Mail order	tertiary	2	purpose built	Yes		Large site	Secondaryurity	large	500	2500
John Menzies		Wholesale news distribution	tertiary	11	adapted	No		Cheap	Small	medium	47	3
Red Oak		Warehousing	tertiary	1	adapted	No		Road access / Central	Traffic	small	2	0
									Employee totals =		**1022**	**2780**
Scandura Textiles		Conveyor belting	secondary	10	adapted	Yes	Cleckheaton	Large / Mway access	Hidden	large	35	5
Valliant		C H Boiler manufacturing	secondary	10	purpose built	No		Road access		large	30	4
Heaton Supply		Hydraulics	secondary	12	purpose built	No		Mway access / Market		medium	30	20
Vanroll Isola		Electrical insulation	secondary	15	purpose built	Yes	Locally	Mway access	Out of town	large	30	25
Spring Bathrooms PLC		Bathroom Manufacturer	secondary	9	purpose built	Yes	Halifax	Large / Mway access		large	200	150
Sas Sencor	Euroway Trading estate	Aluminium stockist	tertiary	3	adapted	No		Large site		large	10	1
Debeaux Fairfreight		Import / Export	tertiary	1	adapted	Yes	Locally	Large/ Mway access		large	7	1
Hancocks		Wholesale confectionary	tertiary	9	purpose built	No		Mway access / market		large	6	17
Alpha		Car accessories	tertiary	12	purpose built	Yes	Locally	Mway access		large	22	22
Hill Hire		Commercial Vehicle Hire	tertiary	7	purpose built	No		Mway access		large	22	9
Company Image Ltd.		Clothing	secondary	4	purpose built	Yes	Locally	Mway access		medium		
Artisan Tiles		Tile manufacturer	secondary	2	purpose built	No		Similar firms		medium	60	40
Parcel Force		Delivery	tertiary	7	adapted	No		Mway access		large	62	8
Atlas		Crane hire	tertiary	14	purpose built	Yes	London	Mway access / grant		large	24	24
Dana		Auto parts	tertiary	4	purpose built	Yes	Locally	Mway access / competition		medium	14	6
Maccess		Auto accessories wholesale	tertiary	3	adapted	Yes	Locally	Mway access		medium	13	7
									Employee totals =		**572**	**357**
Unipro Holdings		Computer software	quatemary	3	purpose built	Yes		Central		small	23	17
Bradford Univ. Research		Bus. consultancy	tertiary	3	adapted	Yes	University	University		small	3	1
Stylus Graphics		C.A. design / advertising	quatemary	10	purpose built	No		University / Mway access	expensive	small	7	1
Performance Software		Computer software	quatemary	2	adapted	No		University	access	small	10	5
Unibit Software		Computer software	quatemary	3	adapted	Yes	Locally	Airport access / central		small	23	17
Gane International		Computer software	quatemary	5	purpose built	No		University	building	small	9	2
Beacon Controls		Computers / control systems	quatemary	10	purpose built	Yes		Road access / pleasant		small	17	5
B U S S	Listerhills Science Park	Computer software	quatemary	10	purpose built	Yes	University	University / pleasant	expensive	small	9	8
Fibre Optic Transmissions		Communications research	quatemary	5	adapted	Yes	Bromley (Kent)	Other firms		small	13	1
Elonex		Computers	quatemary	8	purpose built	No		Central	secondaryurity	small	12	2
Comlink Systems		Computers	quatemary	5	adapted	No		Other firms	expensive	small	2	1
Mainder		Computer Hardware Develop	quatemary	4	adapted	No		Pleasant / central		small	5	5
Advanced Methods & Tools		Comp. software consultants	quatemary	10	purpose built	Yes	University	University		small	4	2
Singleton		Architects	tertiary	3	purpose built	No		Pleasant		small	1	2
OHS		Hygiene and Pollution control	tertiary	10	adapted	No		Pleasant	small	small	5	5
B.T. Secondaryurity		Secondaryurity systems	tertiary	5	adapted	No		Central		medium	7	1
Loma		Quality control systems	tertiary	9	purpose built	Yes	Farnborough	Central / Mway access		small	20	2
Donnelly UK		Marketing	tertiary	6	purpose built	Yes	Cleckheaton	Central / Mway access	secondaryurity	medium	60	30
Memory Assessment		Clinic	tertiaryiary	4	adapted	Yes	University	University	expensive	small	5	5
									Employees		**235**	**112**

Fig 5.14   *Details of Bradford's industry*

TASK BOX

Data representation (see panel over page)

1. Locate proportional graphs or symbols to show the nature of industry at each of the three sites recorded.

2. Annotate the map to highlight those location factors which dominate each site.

3. (a) Draw a single triangular graph to compare the proportions of secondary, tertiary and quaternary industry in each of the three areas.
(b) On the graph, plot the mean figure for all areas.

TECHNIQUES PANEL

Database analysis techniques: looking for trends, patterns, comparisons, and links

Databases are a very useful tool for investigating geographical information. This example is best analysed graphically whilst the one in section 6.7 can be better analysed cartographically and statistically. A good plan is to pose some simple questions, decide which data answers them, analyse the data, and draw conclusions.

E.g. How do the sites vary in nature? Consider locations, premises, type, category, etc
What patterns of employment are there? Consider type, number, gender, etc
What factors influence location and migration? Consider advantages and drawbacks.

A data-map of industry in Bradford

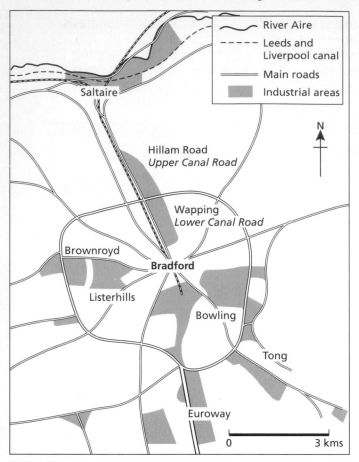

Fig 5.15   *Bradford's industrial areas*

TASK BOX

Decision-making and review

Using the resources in this chapter and the field work database provided opposite, your class - a firm of Business Consultants - must present a report for your top six clients, all of whom are looking for new business sites in Bradford. They are:

A chain supermarket
A micro electronic firm
A food processing firm
A packaging company
A mail order company
A large DIY retail outlet

Divide the work amongst yourselves, and prepare for a formal presentation, using an OHP and 'handouts' at which you:
(i) give a brief summary of the three main sites
(ii) analyse location factors at each site
(iii) comment on the firms there and their views about each site
(iv) try to anticipate likely future operational problems and/or opposition to expansion
(v) allocate premises to each of your six clients, and justify your choice of sites.

TECHNIQUES PANEL

Data representation

One very effective way of showing data clearly and geographically is by using graphs or proportional symbols, located on a map.

Circles are a common choice, but calculation is awkward based on πr^2. However, there is a simpler, though less accurate graphic method.
i. draw a scale line that covers the range from your smallest to your largest value

ii. draw above the line the smallest and largest sizes of circles you want to use, at the appropriate value of each

iii. draw a second line to touch the top of each circle, to give you the sizes of all the intervening circles

iv. transfer each circle to the enlarged map

v. an added advantage of circles is that they can be easily made into pi charts
e.g. proportional pi charts for each of the six sites based upon the total number of employees and the proportion of males to females

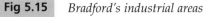

Scale line for number of employees

Another way of showing data made up of three components is to use a triangular graph:
i. convert your three figures into percentages

ii. working clockwise, find the figures on the axes plotting where all three values meet

iii. repeat for each set of figures using an enlarged copy or on isometric paper
e.g. a triangular graph of the Brownroyd site showing the proportion of firms in each sector

Secondary   5 (45%)
Tertiary   6 (55%)
Quaternary 0
Total   =   11 (100%)

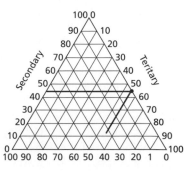

Quaternary (% of firms in each sector)

Key Ideas and Concepts	General Skills	Geographical Techniques
• A divided estuary • The changing dockland • Waterfront renaissance • Inner city redevelopment • Indicators of deprivation • Housing enquiry • Planning for the future	• Data analysis • Mapping skills • Data representation • Database handling • Statistical analysis • Fieldwork activities	• Annotated maps • Aerial photo analysis • Sketch plans • Choropleth mapping • Spearman Rank Correlation • Dispersion diagrams • Significance testing

6.1 A divided estuary

The economic logic of Humberside would seem to suggest that the area with its river and shops pointing directly toward Europe is essentially one region. But as recent political events have again shown, the two sides of the estuary remain apart.

6.2 The changing dockland

This chapter looks at the changing nature of the docks and city of Hull on the northern shore. Cargo totals at Hull docks in 1994 were the highest for 30 years and the third best in the port's history. This transformation has come about because of huge investments in facilities, a growing confidence by business, and the increasing conviction that Hull is well placed to become a dynamic European maritime city. Hull currently has one of the best equipped waterfronts in the UK, and handles 10 percent of its trade.

The port of Hull - a brief history

Hull's earliest record as a port is in the twelfth century. Whaling flourished in the sixteenth century, but only in the 1770s were the first docks excavated. Fishing became prominent in the 1850s as the Dogger Bank was discovered and the smoked fish trade became centred on Hull. Rival ports existed at Goole and Beverley. Trade and industry suffered heavily from the bombing in World War II. In the 1960s, Hull was the fourth port in the UK. Though there were still 160 trawlers registered, Grimsby had more and deepwater cargoes were going to Immingham. The list of imports was very similar to those of today and Europe was the main export market with manufactured goods dominating.

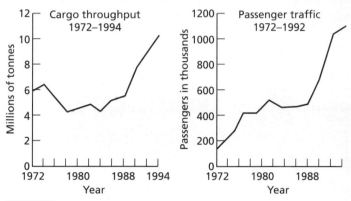

Fig 6.1 *Cargo and passenger trends through Hull docklands from 1972-1994*

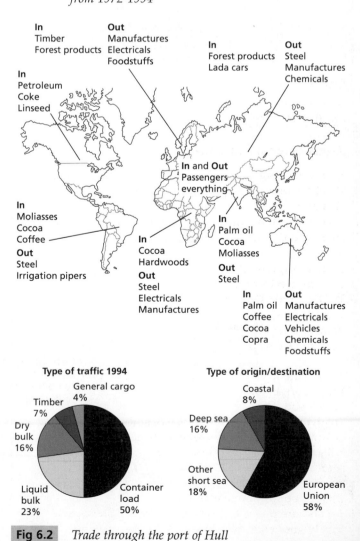

Fig 6.2 *Trade through the port of Hull*

TASK BOX

The changing docklands

1. Use the maps from Chapter 1, an atlas and the resources on these two pages to draw a large sketch map of the port's location, which you can annotate throughout this work.

2. Summarise the traffic patterns (trends, goods and places) of Hull in 1994.

3. Explain how and suggest why Hull has managed to regain its position as a major British port.

6.3 *The waterfront renaissance*

The regeneration of the London docklands was seen by many in the 1980s as the most important inner city development in Europe. It was offered opportunities for residents, investors and businesses, close to the city centre. It brought environmental improvement and waterfront recreational and leisure facilities.

In a similar but smaller way, Yorkshire's famous port and historic city is now enjoying a Renaissance in its fortunes. Along the seven miles of waterfront, shopping streets have been paved over, buildings restored, old warehouses brought back to life, and major projects like a Marina, a shopping centre and a leisure complex have grown up on formerly derelict areas.

Smith & Nephew's transformation

In the 1850s, a local firm launched its medical business in Hull when pharmacist T J Smith and his nephew Horatio moved the company to Neptune Street, Hessle Road, and began manufacturing wound dressings and bandages.

But the latest good news for the city of Hull is that Smith & Nephew PLC is investing a huge £41.3 million in the site over the next five years, including a £2.65 millions Regional Selective Assistance grant from the DTI.

Named 'Project Neptune', this represents the largest single capital investment in the history of the company and will transform the company's medical division on the Hessle Road.

Fig 6.3 *The attractions of Priory Park*

Priory Park set to fulfil potential

Priory Park, the region's fast-developing premier business park.

Offers an excellent strategic and access to national and international transportation links. Regional Selective Assistance as the site enjoys Assisted grants are a further incentive to move here.

TASK BOX

Waterfront renaissance

1. Draw a large sketch plan of the waterfront area (see Figure 6.4), classifying the developments as port-based, other industrial and retail/leisure

2. State the developments and analyse the location factors at work in the four examples on these pages - Hessle Road, Priory Park, the Town Docks and Salt End - consider costs, land, grants, workforce, accessibility, markets and geographical inertia

---

Fig 6.4 *The western docks*

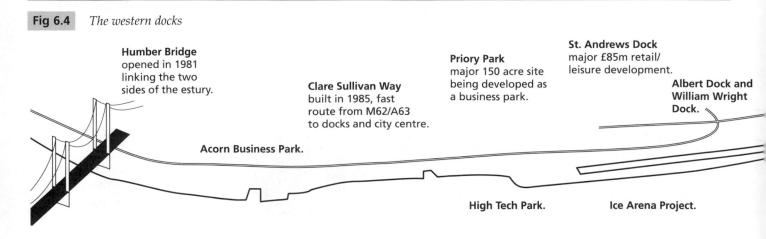

Humber Bridge opened in 1981 linking the two sides of the estury.

Clare Sullivan Way built in 1985, fast route from M62/A63 to docks and city centre.

Acorn Business Park.

Priory Park major 150 acre site being developed as a business park.

St. Andrews Dock major £85m retail/leisure development.

Albert Dock and William Wright Dock.

High Tech Park.

Ice Arena Project.

CITY OF HULL - WATERFRONT RENAISSANCE

In the 1970s, Hull City Council bought up the failing Town Docks and began developing them as a symbol of the city's 'waterfront renaissance'.

The two docks within the Marina have helped to attract property development around the city centre. The 10-acre site provided yachting services, a four-star hotel, housing, and apartments in the converted 'Warehouse 13'.

The area boasts a Maritime Heritage Trail.

The third dock became the spectacular Prince's Quay shopping centre, built within the dock on steel piles driven into the water. A regional centre itself, it attracts numerous tourists including over 500 coach parties a year.

The historic Old Town area nearby has benefited from a variety of grants.

Hull's own Golden Mile

The Giant Hull works for BP Chemicals is one of North Humberside's biggest industries, employing more than 1000 directly and providing work for many more through outside contractors.

The mile-long site has a production capacity of 1.5 million tonnes of chemicals a year, most of its output going into other industries for processing into consumer products including food, clothing, paints, plastics, medicines, adhesives and agricultural chemicals.

With sales of products currently running at around £350 million a year, the plant accounts for four per cent of the wealth created in Humberside each year. The Salt End site is the largest producer of acetic acid - vinegar - in Europe.

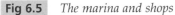

Fig 6.5 *The marina and shops*

Fig 6.6 *The golden mile in Hull*

Hull tidal surge barrier built in 1980 to protect Hull river area from flooding.

Myton swing bridge allows road access to the Eastern docks.

Alexandra Dock handles timber and bulk cargoes.

King George and Queen Elizabeth Docks major £85m investment in passenger ships and terminal by North Sea Ferries and ABP since 1987.

Salt End BP's massive acetic acid plant is the largest in Europe.

Victoria Dock Company formed in 1987 as the site of a £60m housing development.

Riverside berth First of three new Ro-ro berths in the main river to avoid having to use the gates. Part of a £30m programme.

Hull container terminal.

A guide to successful fieldwork in docklands

Instructions

We are booked in for a tour of the Docks. Meet Mr Underwood of Associated British Ports at Port House by 10.30 am. His tour will last about one hour. Use the maps and enquiry questions you have been given already. You must stay on the coach. Photos are permitted where it is safe. Do ask questions and make brief notes. There will be some leaflets to take away. A video about the docks is also available.

The port's new high capacity quayside cranes working a cargo of cocoa beans imported from West Africa

A cargo of Egyptian new potatoes being discharged at Alexandra Dock

Alexandra Dock timber terminal has attracted a number of new shipping lines to the port since the Dock re-opened in 1991

A student's notes, 19 October 1995

1. ABP has been a private company since 1983

2. In 1989, the government ended the National Dock Labour Scheme and this has meant that there is now increased competition and efficiency

3. ABP handles 25% of UK trade in this and its 21 other port operations in the UK

4. Hull has a throughput of 10.25 million tonnes a year, which is 10% of UK trade

5. North Sea Ferries carry over one million ferry passengers a year

6. Links all over the world but the Baltic ports and Rotterdam dominate

7. Docks are limited by tides, need for dredging, and lock width and through time

8. New riverside Ro-Ro berth has eliminated these limitations. Two more are planned at £12 million each

9. ABP have 5 sites to develop (ideally for the manufacturing if imported raw materials) the largest being 10 acres

10. Developments like St Andrews Dock retail and leisure development have created valuable capital

11. Container (or Lo-Lo traffic) is growing rapidly (170,000 units in 1994) and has room to expand

12. ABP has already invested £25 million since 1989

13. Port control has 24-hour satellite, radio, and radar systems

Passengers waiting to embark the ferries to Rotterdam and Zeebrugge at the Princess Margaret Passenger Terminal

The Port of Hull has a growing reputation as a general cargo port as illustrated by this consignment of pipes being shipped to North Africa

A deep sea cargo of bulk animal feed being discharged at the port's bulk terminal in Queen Elizabeth Dock

North Sea Ferries superfreighter m.v. 'Norbank' alongside River Terminal 1, the first of three riverside roll on/roll off terminals to be constructed in Hull

Night time working at the Hull Container Terminal with containers being loaded on a vessel bound for Rotterdam

6.4 Inner city Re-development

In 1977 the Government White Paper 'Policy for the Inner Cities' allowed many cities like Hull to begin to redevelop their inner areas. There was a desperate need to deal with a number of underlying long-term problems. The derelict docklands, uncompetitive industry, high rates of unemployment, poor housing stock and low levels of social and community provision, were all symptomatic of the city's economic and urban decline.

Since 1979, the Inner Area Programme (IAP), now called Urban Programme, has spent over £56 million on 1360 major projects, as well as funding numerous smaller schemes. Using this money (75 percent from central government), Hull city council and its various partners have worked to develop four main sectors: economic; environmental; social; and housing (ended 1991/2).

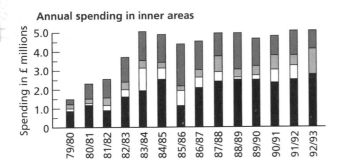

Annual spending in inner areas

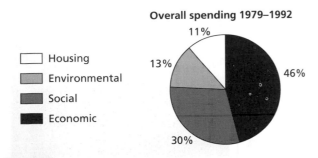

Overall spending 1979–1992

☐ Housing
▨ Environmental
▩ Social
■ Economic

11%
13%
46%
30%

| **Fig 6.7** | *Hull's expenditure of IAP money* |

The economy

The decline of Hull's traditional industries of timber, engineering, and fishing has meant that a very large proportion of the IAP money has been used to retain and develop employment. This list included new factory units, building renovations, training schemes, small business services, and in excess of 600 new jobs.

The Old Town area in particular has seen exciting developments using a wide variety of grants. IAP, Urban Development, Urban Regeneration, Derelict Land, European Regional Development Fund and Housing Association grants have been used alongside private finance. The Marina, the Princes Quay shopping centre and the Trust House Forte Hotel all testify to the area's considerable success.

The £26 million dual carriageway built in 1985 links the docks and the city centre to the M62, while the North Orbital road has allowed the CBD to be pedestrianised.

The environment: Environmental improvement has been vital to encourage development in the city. Using Derelict Land grants, the city has sought to change people's perception of the city.

Housing: Housing stock, especially those dating from before 1919, were in a poor state of repair and with few amenities. IAP money is not easily directed into housing, but the city has tried to tackle these problems.

Social: Inner city areas inevitably contain a high concentration of low income groups with poor social conditions. IAP funding has supported a variety of voluntary and community organisations. Recreation and leisure centres like East Hull baths are important in areas otherwise short of such facilities.

TECHNIQUES PANEL

Choropleth mapping and dispersion diagrams

Choropleth or density shading maps are used in geography to show patterns across an area: e.g. population density, housing characteristics or socio-economic indicators. The lighter the colour used the lower the density. Before this can be drawn, a decision about the categories of data must be taken. There are two methods, both of which involve drawing a dispersion diagram.

(1) draw a scale line to cover the range of data and plot against it the data you wish to use.

Either

(2) find the median (middle value) and divide the items into 'quartiles' to give you 4 categories

Or

simply use 'natural breaks' in the dispersion, to group the data

(3) shade in each area on the map according to the colours chosen

(4) don't forget a key

Upper quartile — 50

Upper middle quartile

Median —

— 25

Lower middle quartile

Lower quartile

— 0

TASK BOX

Inner city redevelopment

1. (a) Describe briefly the changing pattern of IAP expenditure in Hull from 1979 to 1992.
(b) Suggest reasons for the overall pattern of priorities.
(c) What amenities and facilities did Hull gain from this finance?

6.7 Indicators of deprivation

Census returns such as those in 1991 provide evidence of numerous population characteristics. One section of these refers to indicators of urban deprivation.

Fig 6.11   *Map and data following the 1991 census*

TASK BOX

Deprivation

1. Look at the census data below
(a) Compare the city with the rest of England (columns 1 and 2).
(b) Working as a group, copy base maps of the 20 wards.
(c) Divide up the rows and produce a series of choropleth maps to show the pattern of deprivation. Discuss the importance of these indicators.
(d) Explain what the maps show.

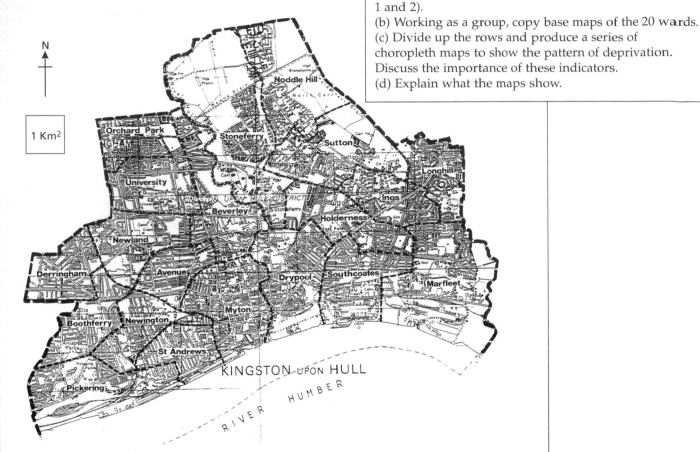

1991 Census (Crown Copyright)	ENGLAND	HULL	Avenue	Beverley	Boothfarry	Derringham	Drypool	Holderness	Ings	Longhill	Marfleet	Myton	Newington	Newland	Noodle Hill	Orchard Pk	Pickering	St Andrews	Southcoates	Stoneferry	Sutton	University
Total Residents	47.055m	254,117	12,328	12,914	12,144	12.630	13,225	13,063	11,521	11,367	11,698	10,907	13,280	11,695	15,657	14,583	9,231	10,901	13,862	15,244	16,001	11,866
Indicators of Deprivation																						
% of residents unemployed	4.5	6.9	6.2	5.1	3.6	4.3	6.1	5.6	6.3	6.8	8.5	12.1	7.9	3.1	9.8	9.7	6.6	11.2	7.1	5.9	5.4	7.7
% of res. on a Govt. scheme	0.6	1.1	0.9	0.8	0.5	0.7	1.1	1.1	1.1	1.3	1.5	1.3	0.9	0.7	1.4	1.7	1.1	1.2	1.1	1	1.2	1.3
% of res. in Social Class V	3	5.3	2.3	3	1.4	4.4	6.6	5.1	5.8	7.6	7.5	6.7	4.1	3.9	6.8	7.5	7.4	7.3	5.2	3.9	3.8	7.3
% of res. in households with no car	23.9	42.4	32.7	27.7	28.3	32.7	39.9	33.3	43.2	45.6	59.9	62.1	46.6	25.2	59.6	58.7	44.9	59.2	45.7	29.9	31	46.7
% of res. in hhds that lack/share amenities	0.3	1	2.6	1.1	1.3	2	1.3	0.5	0.2	0.1	1.9	0.5	1.7	0.8	0.1	0.9	0.6	1.6	1	0.4	0.1	1.1
% of res. in overcrowded hhds	4.5	5	3.4	2.8	2.6	3.2	3.4	4.5	3.2	5.1	9.2	4.2	6	2	8.6	7.6	4.8	6.7	6.4	4.7	3.3	7.7
% of res. in single parent hhds	4	6.2	3	2.8	2.2	2.3	3.8	6.1	3.5	5.7	10.8	5.2	6	2.5	14.4	12.7	5.2	8.4	6.9	5.8	4.1	9.7
% of res. who were lone pensioners over 70	3.2	3.2	3	2.5	5.4	5.9	3.2	2.9	4	2.6	2.4	5	2.5	4.3	2.2	2.8	3.8	3.5	2.3	1.2	3.1	3
% of res. in hhds with limiting long-term illness	11.9	14.1	10.9	10.9	13.4	15	13.2	12.1	19.8	17	15.9	20.4	13	12	13.2	16.2	15.6	16.2	12.1	10.4	13	14.8
% of res. with L.L.T. illness and alone/ with child	3.9	4.4	3.6	3.3	4.6	5.4	4.3	3.1	5.7	4.7	4.2	9.4	3.9	4	4.5	5	4.4	6.7	3.2	2.4	3.7	4.4
% of res. in hhds spaces not self-contained	0.6	0.4	2.0	0.7	0.1	0	0.3	0.1	0.1	0	0	0.8	1	0.1	0	0.1	0	1.1	0.3	0	0.1	0.1
Hull deprevation score (sum of indicators)	60.4	90	71.5	60.7	63.4	75.9	83.2	74.4	92.9	96.5	121.8	127.7	93.6	58.6	120.6	122.9	94.4	123.1	91.3	65.6	68.8	103.8
Housing Characteristics:																						
% of hhds owner-occupied		49.4	66.1	76.6	70.2	60.8	65.5	65	39.6	37.5	24.6	17.2	58.8	77.4	13.7	20.1	48.3	35.8	56.5	61.6	53.7	38.1
% of hhds renting from city council		37.2	4	4.4	17.6	22.5	15.8	26	54.6	58.3	60.8	49.7	21.7	9.4	81.7	76.4	41.8	41.5	34.2	33.6	41.1	52.4
% of hhds renting from others		13.4	29.9	19	12.2	16.8	18.7	9	5.7	4.1	14.6	33.1	19.4	13.2	4.6	3.5	9.9	22.7	9.3	4.8	5.2	9.5
% detached		2.3	1.6	3.8	1.8	1.9	2	4	4.1	1.7	1	0.6	0.9	4.6	0.4	0.8	1.5	0.4	1.3	2.9	9.5	1.9
% semi-detached housing		19.2	4.3	26	24.5	16.6	19	43	21.8	33	14.2	2.9	9.1	24	1.9	14.6	15.9	7.8	22.3	32.5	26.9	24.4
% terraced housing		62.6	66.4	56.5	62.7	77.1	63.6	50	58.7	51.7	76.2	36.1	75	64	81.5	64.8	71.3	50.6	68.4	57.3	53.4	67.4
% flats and other dwellings		15.8	27.7	13.7	11	4.4	15.4	3	15.4	13.6	8.6	60.4	15	7.4	16.2	19.8	11.3	41.2	8	7.3	10.2	6.3

Planning a coastal enquiry	General Skills	Geographical Techniques
• Open learning • Setting the scene • What physical processes are at work? • What are the issues that result? • How successful is existing management? • What are the other management options? • What should be done?	• Research skills • Data analysis • Values analysis • Management and environment planning • Environmental Impact Analysis • Cost-benefit analysis • Decision-making	• Annotating maps • Aerial photo interpretation • Sketch mapping • Annotating field-sketches • Systems diagrams • Wind roses • Fieldwork

7.1 A coastal enquiry - an open learning assignment

The aim of this chapter is to enable you to research, understand and become familiar with an extended stretch of coastline. It gives you some headings and questions but it is only a framework within which to work. Plan and discuss what you are doing with your teacher/lecturer. You may decide to work alone or share tasks to produce a booklet. Include people's views as well as factual information. Use description, explanation, and analysis. Use diagrams and labelled sketches not just written work. Investigate the nature of the coast, the processes at work, the issues involved, and the attempts being made to manage it.

You may be able to visit this area to collect your own primary fieldwork evidence, or write to organisations for secondary information. If not, there is a range of resources here.

Researching further information is an important part of any assignment. This can be via books, scientific magazines and newspapers, or by using CD-Roms. You could also use IT skills in your data handling and in your final presentation.

TASK BOX

Setting the scene

Where is this area? Map its location. What is it like? Look through this chapter and identify briefly the range of physical features found in this area. Use an Atlas, an OS map and Chapter 1 to identify the places, the land uses, the population density, and the economic activities that make up its geography. What seems to be the main issues here? How serious are they? Answers could be in brief bullet point notes or be annotated on to a large sketch map, or a series of smaller maps.

Research extension task using CD-Roms
Using these names, key words, dates, sources, etc.
Holbeck Hall Hotel, Scarborough: June 3rd-8th 1993, Earthflow: cliff fall: slide: slump: Scarborough Evening News: Yorkshire Post: National papers ...

7.2 Setting the scene

Twenty-nine villages have fallen into the sea over the last one thousand years, along just one forty mile stretch of our coast. This part of the Yorkshire coast, from the cliffs of Flamborough Head, through the plain of Holderness, to the Humber estuary, has a variety of features and processes that show how our coastline is continually changing.

HOLDERNESS NEEDS HELP

Fig 7.1 *The issue. Holderness Advertiser, 17 March 1994*

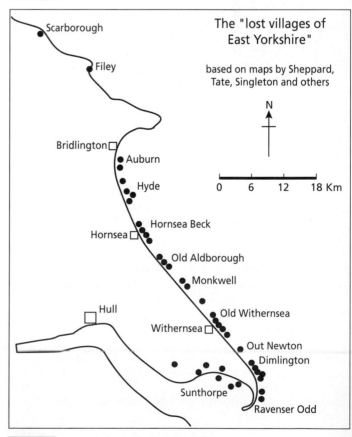

Fig 7.2 *The lost villages of East Yorkshire*

7.3 The physical processes

Coasts of accretion, e.g. Humber (estuary) and Spurn Head (Spit)
'The deposition of sediment along shorelines in sheltered low energy environments.' Spilling and surging breakers are constructive in nature and help to form protective beaches along our coastlines.

Coasts of erosion, e.g. Flamborough Head (chalk headland) and Holderness (boulder clay coast)
'The wearing away and removal of material by sea and land processes along shorelines, in exposed or high energy environments.' Differential erosion is seen when waves erode resistant rocks slowly, whilst nearby softer rocks are removed rapidly. Plunging breakers are destructive and remove beaches.

Coasts of submergence, e.g. all of this section of coastline
'The world-wide rise in sea level resulting from global warming means that low-lying coastal areas will be increasingly at risk from flooding.' The Humber estuary would be effected and neighbouring coastlines would also become more easily damaged by storms, as their existing defences would be inadequate.

Fig 7.3

Houses at Barmston may have worsened the problem

Figure 7.4: Erosional environments can be divided into 2 types

(1) Cliff-foot or marine processes
- Tidal currents with their strong diurnal movements have both a vertical and horizontal impact. These move large amounts of water and sediment rapidly, as well as shaping the sea bed. They are a major cause of flooding. Tidal scour often concentrates erosional activity in estuaries.
- Wave energy is the result of wind action, and the fetch is the distance over which winds have built up the wave height. Depth of water, effects of longshore drift, the angle of wave attack, the resistance, lithology and structure of rocks are also important. The processes of sea erosion by waves are:

hydraulic action – wave pressure forces air into rock joints and this helps remove rock fragments,

abrasion (corrasion) – waves throw material against cliffs,

solution (corrosion) – rocks such as chalk or limestone are dissolved by weak acids or salt.

(2) Cliff-face or terrestrial processes
- Cliffs may be weathered by chemical and mechanical processes, and the resulting material is then moved by gravity. This series of processes is called mass movement, and can be divided into various categories.

Rockfalls – material falls down to the foot of the cliff

Landslides – saturated material slips seawards along a slip plane (see Figure 7.5)

Rotational slips, slumping and mudflows – all result from the increasing effects of water content, created by heavy rain or a spring. Each of these is progressively less stable and less predictable.

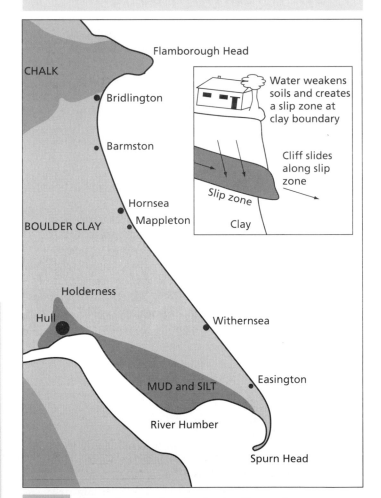

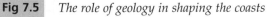

Fig 7.5   *The role of geology in shaping the coasts*

TASK BOX

The physical processes

Using the information about the coast from Holbeck Hall to the Humber estuary, on this and the next two pages, identify the processes at work and explain how and why they vary along this coastline. Draw annotated sketches, diagrams, and maps as well as written work. You should refer to the places most affected by each process.

The length of the 'spokes' indicate, (as a percentage) how often the wind blows from that compass direction. eg there is a north wind 6% of the time

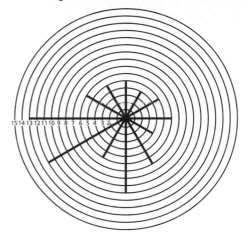

Fig 7.6   *Directions of prevailing winds*

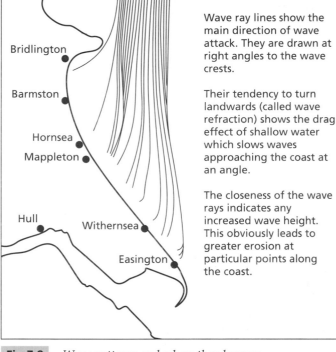

Wave ray lines show the main direction of wave attack. They are drawn at right angles to the wave crests.

Their tendency to turn landwards (called wave refraction) shows the drag effect of shallow water which slows waves approaching the coast at an angle.

The closeness of the wave rays indicates any increased wave height. This obviously leads to greater erosion at particular points along the coast.

Fig 7.8   *Wave patterns and where they happen*

Spurn under threat

Old maps of Spurn show that it has been destroyed by storms at various times in its history. It seems to grow too long and the narrow neck section is breached by waves, creating an island. Later, it begins to form again, always further west. This happened in 1360, 1608, 1849, and 1953. In February 1996, north east winds from a depression in the North Sea drove waves through the neck, temporarily cutting the road with Spurn Point. Is this a prelude to further breaches and isolation?

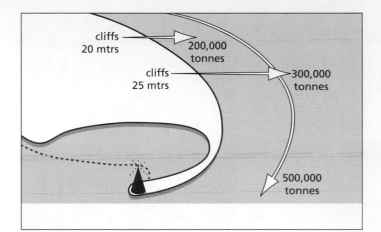

Fig 7.7   *Chalk cliffs at Flamborough Head*

Expert blames 'ords'

Withernsea-born Dr Ada Pringle, a geography lecturer at Lancaster University, is seen as the acknowledged expert on 'ords'. These are distinctive hollows, which form in beaches along this coast. They occur at various points and appear to migrate southwards at a rate of some 0.5 km per year. It seems that localised wave action is concentrated in these hollows and this exposes the soft boulder clay beneath the thick sand or shingle beaches. Once the protective beach is removed, erosion increases.

Dr Pringle's research over 15 years shows that these 'ords' greatly accelerate the rate of erosion. One such hollow is currently active below the cliffs near the village of Easington, whilst others are visible at Hornsea and south of Mappleton.

Fig 7.9   *Spurn Head*

Fig 7.10 *Identify numbered features near Flamborough Head*

The Humber estuary

Geography Professor John Pethick has researched the Humber estuary for nearly 20 years along with his colleagues at Hull University. He has emphasised that there are three different systems operating there. Firstly, there is the river system which drains almost one-fifth of England, and releases some 250 million cu mecs of fresh water into the estuary (more than three times the amount released by the Thames). This also brings with it river sediments and a variety of effluents.

Secondly, there is the coastal system which delivers large amounts of beach sediment into the mouth of the estuary and onto the offshore submarine bars.

The third system, the tide, forces sea water and coastal sediments upstream along the northern shore. This natural process creates salt marshes and mud flats, but it can also obstruct the deepwater channels and allows pollutants to collect. Dredgers and river pilots are needed to allow ships to reach the Humber ports safely.

In winter it is common for deep Atlantic depressions to remain stationary over the North Sea. Before they eventually fill, they can often bring strong north easterly winds, e.g. Jan 1982 and February 1996.

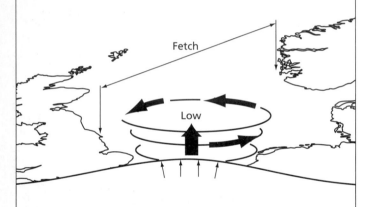

This low pressure causes a definite rise in sea level, which, together with the winds and high tides, can produce 'surge' condition. The resultant 'plunging' breakers remove beach material very rapidly.

Fig 7.11 *The effects of low pressure systems and depressions*

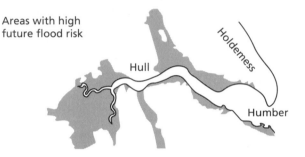

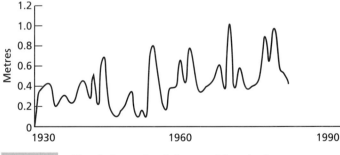

Changes in sea level at Immingham, since 1930

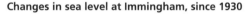

Fig 7.13 *Trends in sea level change at Immingham*

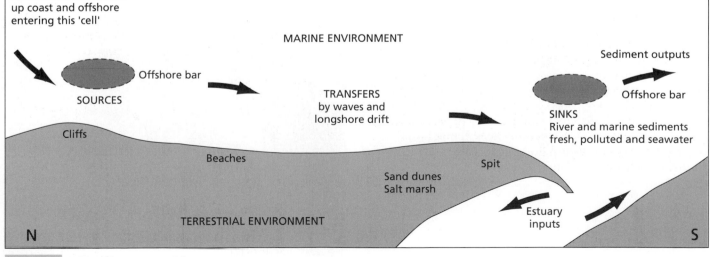

Fig 7.12 *Coastal system model*

7.4 The issues and management

Skipsea

With no help coming from the local council, one landowner has had gabions, wire cages filled with rocks, built in front of the cliffs to protect his caravan park from erosion by waves.

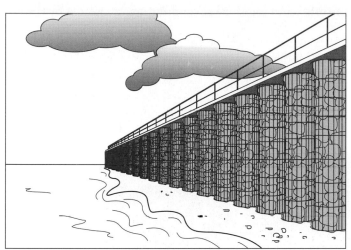

Fig 7.14   *Wire cages stop cliff erosion*

Barmston

> "I used to live on the cliff top and I can remember the winter when the houses fell into the sea. It was a very frightening time."
> Older resident

> "The seaward end of the village is only caravans and a café these days. The houses, the garage, the pub, and other buildings are safe."
> New resident

The erosion rate is now 1.5 m per year. The finer clay is washed out to sea in suspension. The sands and gravels are transported southwards by the very strong longshore drift.

Fig 7.15   *Views of the coast and the problems*

Hornsea

Engineers go for hard defences at Hornsea - (1980)

A report by consultants Lewis and Duvivier, states that the North and south Bastions and the seawalls between are protecting the hotels and 'front' well, and in general the existing groynes are continuing to trap sediment. However, erosion is taking place at the southern end of the town. 'Ords', storm surges, and spring tides, are acting together to create a complex situation.

The Council is advised that further work on groynes and seawalls is urgently needed.

'Strategic retreat' for Hornsea? (Nov. 1994)

Hull University Professor, John Pethick, in his final and controversial report, recommends that resorts like Hornsea be allowed to decline.

This type of approach, increasingly being adopted by planners in the USA, is based on the simple truth that the sea will win in the end. Property owners prepared to move and rebuild inland, were offered 40 percent of the insured value of their property.

The whole problem is one of trying to change people's attitudes. Strategic retreat is not only cost effective, it is better for the environment as it means less unsightly civil engineering.

Fig 7.16   *Hard or soft engineering?*

Hornsea Councillor Mr Brian Spooner dismissed the report as ridiculous, saying "I want my family to live here for generations to come. We need to protect our history."

Fig 7.17   *A new groyne in action*

Council counts the cost at Hornsea - (Aug 1994)

In the 20 years since 1994, Holderness Borough Council has replaced or repaired a total of 19 groynes, underpinned the resort's seawalls, put in a floodwall, and built a new revetment beneath the South Promenade. The design of these works has been deliberately tailored so as not to damage the beach front or deter holiday makers and commercial activities. The groyne involved is also seen in the accompanying photograph, coping with surging breakers, in a heavy sea.
Capital cost: £5 179 130

Residents unhappy with seawall solution - Sept. 1995

Since 1995, Holderness Borough Council has carried out extensive works similar to those at Hornsea. In addition, a new wave return wall, and rock armour from France and Norway, brought in on 4250 tonne barges, should help buttress the exposed foundations of the existing southern sea wall.
Capital cost: £6 297 020
Maintenance cost: £32 000 per year

Residents of the North Promenade
suffer the twice-daily effects of winter storms. Sand and spray can reach as high as third floor windows when waves, wind and tides combine. The value of Withernsea's beach front property continues to fall alarmingly.

Fig 7.18   *Choosing the right scheme*

Groynes

Groynes are structures built at right angles to the shore to protect the cliff foot by retaining sediment otherwise lost to Longshore drift.
Advantages
Locally very effective in holding sand and shingle sediments. A relatively low cost of construction.
Disadvantages
Create scour (erosion) beyond the area protected by the groyne field
Need regular maintenance
Rarely sufficient to solve problems on their own
Interrupt natural course of events along an extended section of coast

Fig 7.19

Changes at Withernsea, 1997

Seawalls

Seawalls are structures built parallel to the shore to protect the cliff foot by deflecting the wave energy.
Advantages
Prevent landward movement of the shoreline
Provide reassurance to local residents or commercial activities
Special shapes can reflect or absorb particular wave types
Absorbent varieties similar to revetments have longer lifespan
Disadvantages
Seen as ugly by holiday makers and conservation groups
High capital costs and periodic maintenance needed
Liable to be undermined by basal scour (erosion)
Local solution only and not suited to an extended section of coast

TASK BOX

The issues

As a class, try to summarise the situation at places along the coast, noting the views of the people and the organisations involved. Draw up a conflict matrix (see the TECHNIQUES PANEL in section 4.5). You could annotate a map to help you remember the issues and the locations concerned. Prepare for a Public Inquiry by collecting facts and ideas for use later on.

Easington

Fig 7.20 *Gas companies threatened by erosion*

Cliff drainage looks promising - (April 1985)

Hull University's experiments have successfully reduced the rate of cliff collapse near Easington. Using drainage trenches to dry out the clay cliffs, there has been a significant reduction in slumping. The key question is whether it would work on a large scale?

Gas companies seek government help - (July 1993)

Both British Gas and BP are concerned about the increasing rate of cliff erosion below their terminals at Easington, triggered by the presence of 'ords' and of cliff collapse during winter storms. As places 'updrift' of Easington build groynes to trap sediment, the threat to the terminals grows.

GOVERNMENT TO APPROVE SEAWALL APRIL 1996
The Dept. of the Environment will soon be approving a controversial one kilometre sea defence to protect the BP and British Gas terminals at Eastington, which now handle 25% of all North Sea gas production. Villagers are angry that there are no plans to protect the village itself. Opinion is split between those who work for the transitional companies, and those residents who feel they are being ignored.
Will M.A.F.F. provide money to extend the sceme?
Capital cost £4,500,000

Spurn Head cut-off - (February 1996)

The small group of lifeboatmen and their families, the coastguard and the Humber pilots are only able to reach the point by boat or four-wheeled drive vehicles at low tide. Gale force winds and high tides have removed a further 200 metres of concrete road. The Yorkshire Wildlife Trust and the Spurn Heritage Coast Project are concerned for the valuable sand dune and salt marsh ecosystems, and the important bird sanctuary that occupy the spit.

Spurn Head abandoned - (October 1995)

Holderness Borough Council decided to abandon Spurn Head to nature, and claims that maintaining road access is too costly.

Spurn Head

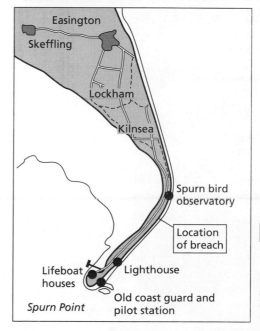

Easington
Skeffling
Lockham
Kilnsea
Spurn bird observatory
Location of breach
Lifeboat houses
Lighthouse
Old coast guard and pilot station
Spurn Point

Fig 7.21

Why do some defences fail to protect sand dunes and salt marshes

7.5 Managing Mappleton: a case study of one village's battle against the sea

As our village sinks slowly into the sea

The tiny hamlet of Mappleton (population 103) perches atop 50 feet cliffs of treacherously soft clay on the Holderness coast between Hull and Bridlington, a region where more than 30 villages have been engulfed by the sea.

Unless something is done quickly, Mappleton is doomed to join neighbouring Sand-le-Moors, Monkwike and Waxholme, once thriving communities that today are no more than rubble on the seabed. Once Mappleton's parish church of All Saints stood three miles from the North Sea. Now it is less than 300 yards. "Another 12 feet vanished in less than a month," says Geoff Porter, 44, as we stand 25 feet away from where his street, Cliff Lane, terminates in thin air. "When we moved here 16 years ago, two other houses stood between us and the sea - and they were 35 feet from the cliff edge. Now we are to be the next to follow."

A steel barrier seals off Cliff Lane. On it is a notice which reads: "Please help us keep Mappleton by the sea - not Mappleton in the sea". It was placed there by Dorothy Meggit, who is co-ordinating the village's fight for survival. She and her husband Jack have lived in Cliff Lane for 33 years.

"Sid Robinson and his wife used to live at the end of the lane in those day," says Dorothy, "But the sea took their house. Mrs Buffey's house was next to go. I'm doing my best to alert everyone to the fact that we're not just losing land - we are losing England."

'PLUS', 1 August 1988

Fig 7.22   *Before the coast was protected*

Mappleton in 1988

The Department of the Environment
There is a real need to protect the B1242 coast road from erosion by the sea, we must act now.

Poeford Duvivier, consulting engineers
Cost for the scheme is estimated at £21 million. Recommended works include the construction of two rock groynes to allow the beach to reform, regrading of the cliffs, and further rock armour at the cliff foot.

Holderness Borough Council
Funding is dependent on 'tourism benefit', so any EU scheme must include an access road, a car park, and toilets.

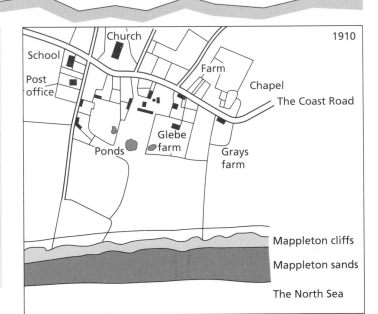

Fig 7.23

Are the new defences working?

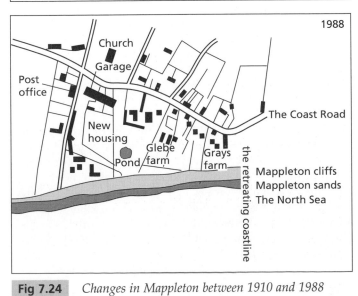

Fig 7.24   *Changes in Mappleton between 1910 and 1988*

TASK BOX

Managing Mappleton

Set out the reasons why Mappleton needed to be protected using the maps and reports overleaf. Describe and explain the coastal management scheme chosen, by drawing a sketch from the aerial photo and annotating it, using the maps to help you. Evaluate the success of the scheme, using resources on this page and an Environmental Impact Analysis.

Geoff and Karen Porter have lost two homes to Holderness cliff erosion and say they are still paying the price.

The building of the £2.1 million sea defences may have stopped the erosion, but visitors spoil their privacy. "All we wanted to do was to save Mappleton, we didn't want it to become a tourist area."

One advantage of the new groynes at Mappleton is the cliff-top residents like the Porters can now once again insure their properties against the sea.

Holderness Advertiser, 3 February 1994

Fig 7.25

Aerial photo of Mappleton

Woman's crusade over crumbling house

A woman whose home teeters on the brink of collapse into the North Sea has launched a rare legal move which could have a huge implication on sea defence schemes across the country.

If Sue Earle succeeds in proving Holderness Council exacerbated her problems by building a defence scheme three miles from her farm, it could open the way for similar claims against other local authorities.

She is taking the council to a Lands Tribunal, citing the 1949 Coastal Protection Act, which says no person should suffer because of coastal protection works undertaken by an authority.

Her home at Grange Farm, Great Cowden, East Yorkshire, stand just feet from crumbling cliffs, and a dairy she ran there fell into the sea earlier this year. Now her garage, which houses the central hearing system, hangs over the cliff edge and she fears the property may collapse before Christmas.

She claims there could have been another fifteen years life in the farm had Holderness Council not built a sea defence scheme at the village of Mappleton, three miles up the coast. "Things have steadily got worse since then and we really are on borrowed time. I think more studies should have been undertaken to see what effect the scheme would have had on those people further down the coast," she said.

Yorkshire Post, 20 November 1995

Fig 7.26   *Not everyone thinks the scheme is so great*

TECHNIQUES PANEL

An environmental impact analysis

An Environmental Impact Analysis (EIA) sets out to estimate the effects of plans that may cause major changes to the environment. It therefore has a different emphasis to a simple cost-benefit analysis (see Sections 3.5 and 7.7).

(1) Select suitable headings for impacts on the natural environment

(2) repeat this for the human environment

(3) prepare a bi-polar grid to score each of these factors (Section 5.5)

(4) impacts may then be totalled, even weighted (Section 4.4), adjustments to the plans made and a final decision taken, e.g.

environmental factors	negative impacts				neutral impacts		positive impacts		
	5 -4 -3 -2			-1	0	1	2 3	4	5
coastal erosion									
sediment accretion									
drainage									
ecology and habitats									
visual factors									
development									
recreation									
employment									
agriculture									
residence . . . etc.									

- Many deciduous woodlands in the Dales are being replaced by coniferous plantations. What are the opportunities and threats created by this decision?
- As upland agriculture comes under increasing economic pressure in the Dales, the Wolds and the North York Moors, what alternatives in business and landscape offers themselves to local people in such areas?

Fig 8.4   *What to do with derelict urban land?*   **Fig 8.5**   *The problem of traffic in our cities*

HONEYPOT LOSES ITS ATTRACTION

Malham, the most visited National Park site in the country by school parties, is one of many of Yorkshire's honeypot locations. Tourism is vital to the economic future of the Yorkshire Dales, but the costs of coping with more than 8 million visitors each year may be becoming greater than the benefits they bring.

Talk to Mrs Boocock, at the Lister's Arms, and she'll point to the importance of tourists in her business (75 percent of trade). The food and drinks she and nearby cafes sell help keep businesses afloat and create much needed local jobs. Without this albeit seasonal and part-time employment, there would be an even greater drift of young people away from the village. The Cove Centre with its sales of souvenirs and outdoor equipment, the local guesthouses and the National Park Visitor Centre (half a million visitors per year), all cater for the tourists.

Others in the village though are less convinced. Farmers like Mr Harrison will tell you of the gates left open, the litter dropped and the dogs allowed to run after sheep. The National Park Officers will point to the £100,000 spent annually in the area on footpath repairs eroded by walkers.

Older residents will bemoan the loss of privacy and the growing traffic and parking problems (up to 300 parked cars locally). Young couples like John and Sally would like to stay in the village, but the arrival of city folk buying up property for retirement, second homes and holiday cottages, is forcing up prices beyond their reach.

The newly defined Yorkshire Dales National Park will have to grapple with these issues and find solutions. Park and ride schemes, artificial footpaths and more car parks may not be enough. Other more radical strategies may be needed. Closing roads and footpaths when parts of the park reach 'carrying capacity' and even charging entry fees, are methods already used in parks in the USA.

One thing is certain, the conflicts will grow and there will be an increasing need to manage the park pro-actively. "What is needed is a sustainable tourism which does not have such a detrimental impact on the environment," says Ray Lonsdale of the YDNP.

Yorkshire Regional Times
Our Threatened Environment series No. 1 - 1 January 2000

TASK BOX

Millenium special Newspaper supplement:

'Our threatened environment'

Group task.
The Editor of the Yorkshire Regional Times has asked your geography group to prepare a special four-page supplement for 1 January 2000 edition of the paper.

It will focus on environmental pressures in the Yorkshire Region. The Editor is especially interested in your perspectives, as 16–19-year-olds, on those issues that will affect you and your families over the next 20 years. Do not be afraid to express controversial views as long as you can argue your ideas with some evidence.

Select an issue and produce an article of no more than 400 words, with an eye-catching headline. The work should be word processed and carefully set out. Include brief interviews and differing viewpoints if you wish. An example is set out above.

Glossary

Accretion — The process of deposition or accumulation of sediments.

Airmass — Region or parcel of air that has distinct characteristics, largely determined by the origin of the air involved, e.g. Tropical maritime

Anticyclone — System in which air diverges and subsides, in such conditions air is warmed and remains stable.

Aquifer — Rock type which allows water to pass through it or be held within it e.g. chalk or some types of sandstone.

Beach nourishment — The importing of sand artificially to replace beach material previously removed by erosion.

Boulder clay (Till) — Material deposited by ice sheets during the Ice Age over many lowland areas of Europe.

Cliff-face processes — Those subaerial (land) processes which operate on cliffs, including weathering, mass-movement and erosion.

Cliff-foot processes — Those marine (sea) processes which operate on cliffs and beaches, including erosion, deposition and transport, by waves, currents and tides.

Cumecs — Standard unit of discharge : cubic metres per second.

Demography — The study of population patterns and characteristics.

Depression — System in which air converges and rises. In such conditions differing air masses are brought together and this produces frontal rainfall.

Derelict land — Land not currently being used economically, though showing evidence of previous usage.

DOL — Dissolved oxygen level ; the lower the value recorded, the greater the level of pollution in river water.

Drought — Period of sustained, abnormal water shortage ; most commonly caused by lack of rainfall.

EA — Environment agency. Formally the National Rivers Authority : government body to monitor rivers and coasts.

Fetch — The horizontal distance over which waves are created by wind action.

Flood abatement — Measures undertaken within a catchment area to alter or preserve the hydrological characteristics to prevent or control flooding.

Flood adjustment — Measures undertaken within a catchment area to cope with the effects of flooding.

Flood protection — Measures undertaken in relation to the river channel to protect from flooding.

Flood recurrence interval — This is an estimate of the likely return period in years of a flood of a particular severity : it is an important insurance and design parameter.

Footloose industries — Industries or firms not heavily constrained by location factors : can be profitable at a range of locations.

Fret — Localised sea mist occurring along Yorkshire coast under the influence of colder sea air beneath a summer anticyclone.

Frontal (cyclonic) rainfall — Rainfall occurring along the line of a front, typically within a trough or depression.

Gabions — Wire or metal cages holding rocks, placed at the foot of cliffs to help protect coasts from erosion by waves.

Geotextile — A specially created fabric that resists erosion yet allows plants to colonise it

Greenfield sites — Land not previously used other than by agriculture or open space : usually at the edge of urban areas.

Gripping — The practice of cutting drainage channels to improve rough pasture.

Groynes — Beach protection device built at right angles to the coast, designed to capture sediment as it moves under the effect of longshore drift.

HAT — Housing Action Trust : one means by which government help for inner cities is targeted on specific areas to enable regeneration.

Heavy metals — Mineral particles such as mercury, cadmium and zinc.

Honeypot — A location or feature where the high degree of popularity creates significant environmental impacts.

IAP — Inner Area Programme : largely government funded redevelopment of inner city sites (1979)

ICZM — Integrated Coastal Zone Management involves a full consideration of social, environmental and financial factors.

Inner City Redevelopment — Re-use of land, in particular for housing, retail and other services.

Kite diagram — Means of showing how the pattern of data changes with distance : popularly % vegetation cover against slope.

Levees — Ridges of sediment parallel to river channels built by rivers as they spill over onto the floodplain.

Lo-lo — Lift on, lift off, e.g. 'container' traffic.

Longshore Drift — The movement of water and sediment parallel to the shore, which results from waves striking the coast at an angle (swash and backwash).

MAFF — Ministry of agriculture, Fisheries and Food.

Mass movement — Series of processes by which material moves down slopes, e.g. rockfalls, landslides, soil creep and earth flows.

MDF — Mean Daily Flow : a measure of river discharge used to compare outputs.

Ofwat — Government watchdog body appointed to monitor the now privatised water companies.

Ords — Low sections of beach linked to longshore drift. They migrate downdrift and cause increased localised erosion of cliffs.

Quaternary — Literally meaning fourth : used in this sense to categorise industries which are based on information and computer technology (hi-tech).

Rain shadow — Area of little or no rain to the lee of hills, where descending dry air prevents precipitation.

Relief (orthographic) rainfall — Rain occurring where hills cause mobile unstable air to rise, triggering precipitation.

Revetments — Similar to seawalls but often built so as to absorb rather than deflect wave attack. May be built of rocks or baffles.

Glossary continued

Ro-Ro	Roll on, roll off : goods in vehicles driven directly onto or off ferries.
Rock armour	Use of large boulders placed to prevent waves reaching vulnerable coastal features or structures.
RSA grants	Regional Selective Assistance grants used by government to promote development in areas of high unemployment.
Set aside	EU policy to reduce overproduction, by which farmers use their land for grazing, woodland, reserve or tourism.
Shakeholes	Funnel shaped hollows in limestone areas that indicate underground caves or water courses.
Slumping	Process by which cliffs collapse when wetted by rainfall or undercut by waves.
Soft (engineering) defences	Coastal management which works to accomodate coastal processes rather than try to prevent them.
SSSI	Site of Special Scientific Interest.
Stable air	Air unlikely to change in character ; especially in terms of rainfall.
Strategic retreat	Decision to stop defending a coastline and plan the future use of the land accordingly. This may be linked to compensation or relocation grants.
Submergence	The process by which the sea is covering more of the land surface : an effect linked to global warming.
Surge conditions	The way in which intense low pressure systems raise the level of a localised area of ocean e.g. North Sea.
Synoptic chart	A map showing the positions and characteristics of meteorological phenomena : popularly seen in TV and newspaper weather forecasts.
Time lag (lag time)	A measure of the time taken for the effects of precipitation to be felt by a river system : usually measured from peak rainfall to peak discharge.
Urban deprivation	Series of indicators that help analyse the economic and welfare conditions of people living in the inner cities.
Wave ray diagrams	Maps which show the pattern of orthogonals, or lines drawn at right angles to the wave crests.
Wave refraction	The way in which wave direction is progressively altered as waves slow down under the effect of shallowing water.
Wave types	Spilling and surging waves move material landwards and steepen beach gradients : plunging waves remove material seawards and reduce beach gradients.
YDNP	The Yorkshire Dales National Park.

Index